Commercial and Popular Music in Higher Education

Commercial and Popular Music in Higher Education brings together working examples of pedagogy in emerging areas of popular and commercial music to offer practical insights and provide a theoretical framework for today's music educators. Written by a diverse group of experts, the eight chapters address a range of contemporary contexts, including digital instrument ensembles, digital audio workstations, hip hop courses, pop vocal performance, rock bands, studio production, and more.

Considering both the challenges and the benefits of integrating commercial and popular music into teaching, the contributors explore how doing so can enhance student learning. The authors show how a constructivist approach to music pedagogy enables student-led, real-world learning in higher education, and consider how diversity, equity, and inclusion intersect with teaching popular music performance. Compiling experiences and expert resources, this book provides a vital framework for all instructors teaching commercial and popular music.

Jonathan R. Kladder is Assistant Professor of Music Education at the University of North Carolina Wilmington, USA.

CMS Pedagogies & Innovations in Music
Series Editor: Eric Hung, Music of Asian America Research Center

The *CMS Pedagogies & Innovations in Music* series consists of short studies and manuals from a variety of music disciplines engaged in pedagogical discovery and innovative approaches to learning, creativity, performance, and scholarship. Serving faculty, administrators, instructors, and future instructors, these short-form books provide new ideas and theories about music curricula in higher education; evidence-based discussions on pedagogical methods and emerging methodologies for teaching music; strategies for improving musical careers; and resources for areas of study outside the traditional Western musical canon.

Commercial and Popular Music in Higher Education
Expanding Notions of Musicianship and Pedagogy in Contemporary Education
Edited by Jonathan R. Kladder

For more information, please visit: www.routledge.com/CMS-Pedagogies-&-Innovations-in-Music/book-series/CMSPED

Commercial and Popular Music in Higher Education

Expanding Notions of Musicianship and Pedagogy in Contemporary Education

Edited by Jonathan R. Kladder

NEW YORK AND LONDON

First published 2023
by Routledge
605 Third Avenue, New York, NY 10158

and by Routledge
4 Park Square, Milton Park, Abingdon, Oxon, OX14 4RN

Routledge is an imprint of the Taylor & Francis Group, an informa business

© 2023 Taylor & Francis

Library of Congress Cataloging-in-Publication Data
Names: Kladder, Jonathan R., editor.
Title: Commercial and popular music in higher education: expanding notions of musicianship and pedagogy in contemporary education/ edited by Jonathan R. Kladder.
Description: New York: Routledge, 2022. |
Series: CMS pedagogies & innovations in music|
Includes bibliographical references and index.
Identifiers: LCCN 2022006653 (print)|LCCN 2022006654 (ebook)|
ISBN 9781032107196 (hardback)|ISBN 9781032107226 (paperback)|
ISBN 9781003216728 (ebook)
Subjects: LCSH: Popular music–Instruction and study.|
Production music–Instruction and study.|Education, Higher.
Classification: LCC MT18.C665 2022 (print)|LCC MT18 (ebook)|
DDC 780.71–dc23/eng/20220324
LC record available at https://lccn.loc.gov/2022006653
LC ebook record available at https://lccn.loc.gov/2022006654

ISBN: 978-1-032-10719-6 (hbk)
ISBN: 978-1-032-10722-6 (pbk)
ISBN: 978-1-003-21672-8 (ebk)

DOI: 10.4324/9781003216728

Typeset in Times New Roman
by Deanta Global Publishing Services, Chennai, India

Contents

Series Foreword

Welcome to the first volume in the *Pedagogies & Innovations in Music* series published by Routledge, in partnership with the College Music Society. This series includes short studies, manuals, and readers that explore innovative approaches to music teaching in higher education. Books in this series fall into two categories. Some introduce faculty and administrators to new programs and courses that they should consider incorporating into their curriculum, new evidence-based pedagogical strategies that promote greater equity in music classrooms, new approaches to community engagement and creating relevant curricula and programming, and ideas about how to create safer environments that prioritize care and work–life balance. Others are pedagogical materials to be used in courses on underrepresented populations and emerging theories. In the next few years, we hope to have volumes of collected essays on Asian American music, Latinx American music, music and trauma, and music and disability that are suitable for upper-level undergraduates and graduate students. To learn more about the series, including how to submit a book proposal, please visit the Publications section of the College Music Society website (www.music.org).

Eric Hung
Series Editor
Editorial Board
Amanda C. Soto
Nolan Stolz
Mihoko Watanabe

Foreword

Current, relevant, and learner-centered: may all educational experiences provide aspiring music educators with opportunities to actively engage in authentic music making and learning through shared interests and values. Relevant music making through a constructivist process ensures that our students will be prepared to engage with and expand music education. Be inspired by reading this book and connecting with each author's contribution with clear examples of how to expand musicianship and pedagogies in contemporary education.

This book will open the door to active learning in higher education, while connecting with students through their interests and current cultures. Through this process, we also model respect for the individual, as well as the cultures and music making which they represent. Just as sound in our world is accessible to all people, so should music be. When we limit the expansion of how and what to learn in an academic setting, we clearly state, by omission, that it is not valued. Traditionally, what is taught in schools and in universities is seen as "academic," and what is not taught in schools and universities is assumed as "not academic." This has left both large populations and many genres of music outside of learning institutions, and with it the processes in which the music is learned by the very people that make the music. When our programs expand the multiple ways of music making, we demonstrate that all people, music, and cultures are valued.

Music comes with multiple literacies, and to engage in these requires students to actively learn while constructing knowledge and make meaning. Our job in higher education is to continue to expand and demonstrate that we, as educators, will be continual learners. Engaging and remembering the process of learning as adults also provides the opportunity to experience and metacognitively reflect on what it is to learn. This reminds oneself of what it feels like to think, struggle, grow, and empathize as a learner, and to encourage this as a community of continual practice.

Teaching is an art, a culture, a science, and a skill like no other. Through relationships, educators can create a shared community that opens the doors to lifelong learning for everyone. As educators, we were first professional students, and in this experience, we learned firsthand how (and how not) to teach. Throughout my personal experience as a student, I always felt that the traditional *how* and *why* of teaching was missing the most important part – the learners and their values and interests. As our understanding of how the human brain constructs knowledge continues to expand, so must our ability to understand that the industrialized educational experience and systems of the past simply lost the human in what true learning is for each person. A learner-centered education calls upon the individual to construct meaning and understanding, within the context of emotions and processes, that will in turn build the skills and attributes required to become a lifelong learner.

These skills are larger than a mechanical or technical skill, and truly are the traits and habits of an educator that will prepare students for the unknown and to be nimble in thought and practice – at the very least, to remember what it is like to continually learn and grow.

Education is not perfect, as the variable of the human within education is just that, a variable that changes and grows and requires us to be present to the person. We must always be in a process of expanding so we are able to provide the best learning experiences that are open and flexible to what is needed by each individual, for our current and future music education. This is where we see each person – as a capable individual who can construct meaning through their own processes and needs.

An education that is based on a design for the growth of our collective future will provide the skills and mindsets necessary for a relevant music education. So let this book serve as an example of how to engage in authentic learning and music making for all people and cultures, in and through all possibilities of music making. Let this guide us to all that is possible in music education through these examples of how to teach, and the many possibilities in our continued forward movement of music and music education.

Anne M. Fennell, M.Ed.
www.annefennell.com

Preface

We are at a critical point in higher education. Students are emerging from high school with a wider range of skills and knowledge than ever in the past. And, perhaps even more importantly, younger generations of youth can access any information at any time with digital devices – phones, to be exact – from any location in the world. What will we do with this truth? Will we avoid the possibilities that exist in front of us? Will we hide from the technology and the undeniable fact that students – now more than ever – want, or even demand, more autonomy, relevancy, and student-centered learning experiences where they can learn from experts in ways that connect their institutional learning to careers in the music industry?

Opportunities to meet these demands abound. Now it is up to us, faculty in higher education, to change, adapt, or expand the music curricula. It is up to us to embrace what is needed so we can attract and expand the skillset and musical knowledge accepted in higher education. We cannot afford to ignore this need. We must work to expand the music curricula admissions criteria in ways that accept and affirm a wider understanding and definition of musicianship.

This book is dedicated to music faculty who have embraced these truths and continue to advocate for change in higher education. It is also dedicated to those who desire more change and actively pursue pathways to break down racism and elitism in music education that continues to marginalize populations of musicians – specifically, musicians who excel outside the formal institution but have no place to learn music in colleges or universities because we have not created the space for them. Finally, this book is dedicated to those who recognize that we have a problem in music education, a problem of exclusive practices that have existed for far too long, and who are willing to stand out against racism, both in the curriculum and in the music we perform.

May this book offer a new way forward, one that stands as a mechanism to support faculty – and future faculty – who aim to implement new pedagogical approaches and forms of music making needed in higher education.

Jonathan Kladder

Contributors

Adam Patrick Bell is an Associate Professor of music education in the School of Creative and Performing Arts at the University of Calgary, Canada. He is the author of *Dawn of the DAW: The Studio as Musical Instrument* (2018) and editor of *The Music Technology Cookbook* (2020). adam is the principal investigator of the Canadian Accessible Musical Instrument Network (www.camin.network), a group dedicated to making accessible musical instruments, mentoring disability-led music making communities, and manifesting disability perspectives on music making. Prior to his academic career, adam worked as an elementary music teacher by day and music producer by night.

Michael Bierylo is an electronic musician, guitarist, composer, and sound designer. He has been a faculty member at Berklee College of Music since 1995 and is currently Chair of the Electronic Production and Design Department where he led the development of Berklee's Electronic Digital Instrument Program, the Electronic Performance Minor, and the Creative Coding Minor. His major projects include artist residencies with Suzanne Ciani, Nona Hendryx, Hank Shocklee, Richard Devine, Chagall, Robert Rich, and Kaitlyn Aurelia Smith. He is also active in Berklee Online, Berklee's online school, where he authors and teaches music technology courses. He has performed throughout the United States as a member of Birdsongs of the Mesozoic. As a solo electronic artist, he has performed with a laptop computer and modular synthesizers in the US, Berlin, Shanghai, and Krakow, including concerts with Grammy-nominated electronic musician BT and Terrance Blanchard. As an active member of the Audio Engineering Society, he has chaired the Electronic Instrument Design and Applications Track at national conventions, bringing together industry innovators such as Dave Smith and Dave Rossum, as well as design teams from Moog, Roland, and Korg.

Dr. **Radio Cremata** is Associate Professor and Chair of Music Education at Ithaca College. His research has been published in peer-reviewed national and international journals and books. His teaching and research reflect his commitment to innovation, progress, and re-imagining the future of music education. As a teacher, he specializes in music technology education, with an emphasis on non-traditional music education. Programs under his supervision advance student creativities, composition, improvisation, and ear-based musicianship through student-centered learning models empowering students to become co-creators of their educational experiences. He has developed both traditional and progressive programs that have earned him teaching and grant honors. Professionally, he is a keyboard musician versatile in jazz, popular music, and gospel styles. He is also a composer, producer, and recording engineer. His interest in studio production and "real-world" music making has deeply impacted his music teaching philosophy.

Jonathan R. Kladder is Assistant Professor of Music at the University of North Carolina Wilmington. He continues to pursue an active research agenda and is a frequent presenter at local, state, national, and international music education conferences. He is interested in the intersections of music and technology, interrogating the issues of equity and access in undergraduate music admissions, and diversifying the music curricula in ways that enhance creative thinking and music making across the contemporary landscape. His co-edited book *The Learner-Centered Music Classroom: Models and Possibilities* (2020) explores pedagogical models that support learner-centered approaches across the music teaching and learning milieux. His articles have been published in the *Journal of Music, Education, and Technology*, *Music Educators Journal*, *Journal of Popular Music Education*, *Visions of Research in Music Education*, *Creativity Research Journal*, *The College Music Society*, *Contemporary Research in Music Learning across the Lifespan*, and *21st Century Music Education: Informal Learning and Non-Formal Teaching Approaches in School and Community Contexts*. Jonathan is an active musician, playing guitars, keyboards, and MIDI controllers at his home studio in Wilmington, NC.

Dr. **Kat Reinhert** is an accomplished songwriter, vocalist, musician, author, and educator. As a solo artist, she has released five independent albums and sung on multiple projects and recordings for noted artists. She is the former Director of Contemporary Voice at the University of Miami, Frost School of Music, and is a sought-after clinician, speaker, and researcher. She holds a bachelor's in Jazz/Commercial Voice, a master's in Jazz Pedagogy, and a PhD in Music Education, specializing in Popular Music Performance and Pedagogy. She has authored several book chapters and journal articles on contemporary voice and songwriting, and is the immediate past president of the Association for Popular Music Education. She is also the co-founder of Songwriting for Music Educators™, dedicated to helping music educators learn the craft of songwriting. She is currently an adjunct professor at Rider University, NJ, The New School, New York City, and Berklee School of Music, MA. She resides in New York City, where she continues her work on artistic, songwriting, educational, business, consulting, and writing projects.

Oshadhee Satarasinghe is a doctoral candidate in Music Education at the University of Calgary, Canada. She holds a master's degree in Elementary Music Education and a bachelor's degree in Piano and Voice Education, and is certified in both Orff Schulwerk and Kodály pedagogical approaches. In the past 11 years, she has taught elementary music, choral music, private piano and voice lessons, and several university-level courses in both Texas (nine years) and Sri Lanka (two years). She is currently teaching piano and early childhood music lessons in Calgary. She has published several lesson plans that integrate South Asian music into the US music curriculum. She has held multiple workshops at the local and national level on South Asian music integration into the elementary music curriculum. She is very excited to extend her research work in South Asian music integration into Canadian music curricula.

Jazzmone Sutton currently serves as the State Advocacy Engagement Manager for the National Association for Music Education (NAfME). Before joining NAfME as a staffer, she was a passionate elementary music educator and advocate based in North Carolina and past president of the North Carolina Music Educators Association (2021). As an educator, she strived to make her music room a space for all students, with a focus on democratic and student-centered music learning experiences. From various ensembles, collaborative lessons, and performance experiences, she is an advocate for promoting positive learning environments that are inclusive, diverse, and equitable. She maintains her advocacy for music education throughout North Carolina.

Thomas E. Taylor, Jr. is a North Carolina-based drummer and has spent his life discovering drums, rhythms, and music from all walks of life. Brought up in the churches of North Carolina, he came to learn the importance of "supporting the music" from behind the drum set. He studied Classical Percussion and Music Education at the University of North

Carolina Greensboro, where he earned his bachelor's (1991) and master's (2009) degrees. he learned the importance of "swing" playing gigs across the US in the early 1990s. After graduating from college, he began teaching percussion, music, and jazz at community music schools and universities in North Carolina. He spent ten years working, playing, and teaching with world-renowned jazz educator Jamey Aebersold. He continues to teach at North Carolina Central University and the University of North Carolina Greensboro, and performs on the east coast with his drummer-led groups. As an author, he has written articles for *Modern Drummer Magazine* and the *Music Educator's Journal*. He has written a hip hop music appreciation textbook titled *Yo' Check This: Topics in Hip Hop* (2013).

David A. Williams is an Associate Professor of Music Education at the University of South Florida (USF). He joined the faculty at USF in the Fall of 1998 and holds a PhD in Music Education from Northwestern University. His research interests involve the use of learner-centered pedagogies and how these impact teaching and learning in music education. In 2011, he started a live-performing iPad ensemble that is typically made up of five to six musicians, and the band Touch serves as a model of a learner-centered musical ensemble. A typical Touch concert includes music from a wide range of styles, collaborations with vocalists, dancers, actors, and visual artists, as well as significant audience participation.

Introduction

Commercial and Popular Music in Higher Education

Jonathan R. Kladder

Setting the Stage: Commercial and Popular Music in Higher Education

The inclusion of commercial and popular music across the higher education landscape continues to gain momentum in contemporary culture (Birkett, 1992; LoVetri & Weekly, 2003; Parkinson & Smith, 2015). There is evidence of this expansion in scholarly publications, new degree offerings at institutions across the US, and professional development conferences, including the *Association for Popular Music Education, Modern Band Summit*, and *Association for Technology in Music Instruction* (Dyndahl, Karlsen, Nielsen, & Skårberg, 2017; Krikun, 2017; Smith, 2016). "Commercial music," sometimes used synonymously with "popular music," includes the study and performance of music found within the music industry, with direct and purposeful marketed implications for the general public. It often includes entrepreneurial and business techniques aimed at marketing music for consumption by the general public. Commercial music also encompasses the production of music using sound recording technology, home-based recording studios, or digital audio workstations, and is associated with a broad range of music, styles, and genres – all found in popular culture. Similarly, the term "popular music" is "generally used to indicate the diverse range of music genres produced in commodity form for a mass, predominantly youth, market" (Shuker, 2010, p. 1).

The diversity of forms of musicianship represented in commercial and popular music is one of its distinguishing features (Tobias, 2012). For example, musicians in this medium hold a broad range of techniques and skills, as they are often music producers, sound mixing engineers, entrepreneurs, performers, collaborators, and songwriters. They use an assortment of software platforms for the production of music, and perform, record, or produce music using a variety of acoustic *and* digital instruments. Versatility and skill across a range of instruments is a central identifier of musicians in this

DOI: 10.4324/9781003216728-1

medium, including self-taught and ear-based approaches to learning music (Green, 2002; Zollo, 2003). Commercial and popular music comprises a range of genres and styles of music, including bluegrass, pop, R&B, rock, hip hop, rap, country, and many others.

In the US, there are a growing number of music programs that now offer undergraduate degrees in commercial and/or popular music, while others specialize in certifications (Davis & Blair, 2011). These programs continue to expand across the US, as enrollment and demand for relevant degrees in music are more prevalent than ever (Dyndahl, Karlsen, Nielsen, & Skårberg, 2017). For example, a survey of four-year colleges and universities in the US suggests a wide range of music degrees in commercial and popular music are available to prospective students at both public and private institutions (Holley, 2021). Furthermore, prospective students may choose from a variety of bachelor's degrees and certificates, including Bachelor of Science in Commercial Music or Songwriting, Bachelor of Arts in Popular Music or Commercial Music, and Bachelor of Music in Popular or Commercial Music.

Pulling Back the Curtain: Commercial and Popular Music in Music Teacher Education

Although the inclusion of commercial music and popular music in higher education throughout the US has gained momentum, its inclusion in music education, and specifically in music teacher education, has been slow and arduous (Cremata, 2019; Cutietta, 1991; Williams, 2019). Some, such as Cutietta (1991), have argued that it has been a disingenuous integration, stating that "it is rare to find a [music] program that attempts to perform it [popular music] with the authenticity that would be given a Renaissance motet. Instead, it has been forced into our existing formats" (p. 28). Others, such as Kladder (2020), Williams and Randles (2017), and Williams (2019), found that creating spaces for commercial and popular music in the traditional music teacher education curriculum is fraught with challenges and institutional barriers. Sometimes, these barriers are related to institutional policies or credit reductions. In other cases, faculty are resistant to change, and students entering institutions with traditional expectations challenge the notion that popular music is a legitimate form of music making and are unsure whether it should be included in the school curriculum. Others have interrogated its meaning, definitions, uses, and pedagogical practices across cultures and countries from around the world (Cavicchi, 2009; Mantie, 2013; Regelski & Gates, 2009; Welch & Papageorgi, 2014; Williams, 2015). These authors have identified distinct challenges when integrating commercial and popular music in higher education, and specifically in music education, especially within existing traditional frameworks for music learning.

However, even with these barriers, successful changes have emerged in the US that are reflective of greater authenticity than Cutietta's (1991) earlier argument. For example, Powell, Smith, West, and Kratus (2019) suggested that popular music education has gained momentum recently, reflected in three main areas: music education research, curricular change, and the development of non-profit organizations supporting popular music in K–12 and higher education. In music education research, two special research interest groups (SRIGs) have been formed. The National Association for Music Education (NAfME) SRIG for Popular Music Education and the International Society for Music Education SRIG. These groups specialize in researchers who investigate popular music education in both K–12 and higher education contexts. Additionally, some faculty in particular institutions across the US have successfully implemented new courses that teach non-traditional musicianship experiences in music education. For example, at the University of South Florida, a course called *Progressive Music Education Methods* was created as a required course for all undergraduate music education students (Williams & Randles, 2017). Students learn and perform music using non-traditional instruments, often from the popular and commercial music media. In the associated lab, called the *Creative Performance Chamber Ensemble*, students form bands, cover existing songs or write new material, learn music using aural/oral approaches, and experience a variety of instruments (e.g., tablets, MIDI controllers, or guitars).

At Ithaca College, students form bands and learn popular and commercial music in a course called *Contemporary Ensembles in Public Schools.* This is also a required music education course for all undergraduates in the degree program. It meets once a week for one semester. Similar to the University of South Florida, students choose a variety of music making experiences, sometimes using digital technology or popular music instruments. At Montclair State University and the University of Maryland, students learn how to play guitars, drums, and bass guitars in popular music techniques courses. Similarly, at Arizona State University, students gain experience with a range of instruments in a project-based course called *The Art of Teaching Contemporary Musicians*. The University of Southern California's Thornton School of Music offers a one-year immersive master's degree program for prospective music teachers called a *Master's in Contemporary Teaching Practice*, which places emphasis on teaching music beyond the traditional band, choir, and orchestra paradigms. Although curricular change at these institutions reflects an effort by those in higher education to integrate a more expansive and diverse set of music making skills, specifically those outside the Western European art tradition, more expansion is warranted.

Exclusive Audition Requirements in Higher Education

Although the aforementioned institutions highlight changes faculty have made to the undergraduate and graduate music education curriculum, there are challenges associated with auditions as well. Some have exposed a hegemony in the audition procedures used to accept prospective music teachers, suggesting that prospective students are admitted into the teaching profession based on narrow acceptance requirements: the performance of Western Classical music with stringent sight-reading expectations (Kladder, 2021; Koza, 2009). Currently, there are limited music teacher education programs that rely on audition criteria outside the Western European art tradition. Institutional requirements, often set by performance faculty in music programs, focus auditions on stringent sight-reading and performance distinctions in the Western European Art canon (Koza, 2009; Palmer, 2011). This marginalizes many prospective musicians who might become music teachers, but choose other career pathways (Kladder, 2021). Authors have also interrogated the current locus of undergraduate auditions and advocated for the inclusion of commercial or popular music skills or techniques as criteria for admitting students into the music education profession (Cremata, 2019; Kladder, 2020). Others have suggested that the admission procedures currently in place are exclusive, elitist, and racist, with more concerted efforts needed to address issues of access, inclusion, and diversity in the profession (Palmer, 2011; Williams, 2019).

This suggests challenges associated with the integration of commercial and popular music in higher education, however necessary they are, and that currently, the curricular requirements and policies in place create barriers that exist within the profession. And although there is evidence of the emergence and inclusion of commercial and popular music in a few programs across the US, more growth and expansion are clearly warranted (Birkett, 1992; Powell et. al., 2015).

Non-Profit Organizations for Popular Music Education in the US

Beyond higher education, there continues to be momentum and interest for the integration of commercial and popular music in K–12 contexts. For example, since Green's (2002) seminal work with popular musicians, organizations that support commercial or popular music education have emerged. In the US, a non-profit organization called *Little Kids Rock* (LKR) provides

guitars, drums, and keyboard instruments to underprivileged pul
LKR has expanded its focus to offer similar experiences for
music teachers in undergraduate music teacher education progra
vides a variety of fellowships for those interested in teaching po
in higher education. LKR's *Modern Band Higher Ed Fellowship* offers college and university faculty a weeklong training experience to learn guitars,
drums, and keyboards. Attendees share teaching tools and best practices for
implementing new curriculums and showcase syllabuses aimed at supporting new course development for commercial and popular music in higher
education. LKR also offers a *Modern Band* conference that occurs yearly,
involving music teachers from around the US. LKR also supports one-day
training workshops for prospective music teachers, often undergraduate students, with a special focus on playing guitars, drums, and keyboards.

A significant contribution for teaching popular music in US schools
has stemmed from LKR's Modern Band movement. These band programs
have been defined as "a stream of music education that has two simple
guiding attributes: repertoire and instrumentation. The repertoire is what
might typically be thought of as popular music to mean of the people … and
encompasses broad genres of music" (Powell & Burstein, 2017, p. 245).
LKR's Modern Band curriculum is intended to focus on forms of music
that students ideally choose, performing music that "they know and love,
including rock, pop, reggae, hip-hop, R&B, and other modern styles" (Little
Kids Rock, 2021). LKR has offered valuable contributions to the teaching
of popular music in the US.

Pedagogy …? Teaching or Facilitating Popular and Commercial Music

The emergence of popular and commercial music in formal learning contexts raises important questions related to pedagogy – specifically, the
types of instruction used by teachers in the popular music classroom. As
Green (2002) and Jaffurs (2004) found, musicians in this medium often
use informal approaches to music learning: explorational, self-directed,
messy, and often perceived as haphazard. This is confirmed in the process
that Kladder (2021) wrote about in a personal autoethnography, showcasing
the pedagogical differences between his home-based music learning and in-
school music experiences. Others have argued that popular and commercial
music learning is a highly creative process, where musicians write original
songs, experiment with musical ideas, make mistakes, and learn music by
ear (Cremata, 2017). This process is often facilitated, not teacher-directed.
However, what is happening in the formal classroom may be a very different
picture. For example, Byo (2018) examined a popular music program and

found that more time for "mucking around" (p. 266) was warranted. This investigation suggested that although popular music was included in the classroom, learning was primarily teacher-directed and left limited opportunities for students to learn music by ear or improvise, both attributes found central to how popular musicians learn (McIntyre, 2008; 2016; 2019).

In another investigation, Randles (2018) discovered similar outcomes, suggesting that limited time was designated for improvisation or composing in class, where only 32% of teachers surveyed included improvisation. Similarly, 68% of teachers did not include songwriting in the curriculum. Interestingly, these studies reflect a contrast to how musicians in commercial and popular music contexts experience, learn, and perform music (Cremata, 2017; Green, 2002; Jaffurs, 2004). Regardless, continued interrogation of best practices related to the integration and teaching of commercial and popular music in both higher education and K–12 education is warranted. In addition to expanding curriculum and audition requirements in music teacher education programs across the US, this chapter highlights that a key area for consideration, one needing further investigation and inquiry, is pedagogy. As a profession, interrogating pedagogical best practices when integrating commercial and popular music in higher education is critical to culturally relevant music teaching. Specifically, as commercial and popular music continue to emerge in the curriculum, the types of pedagogy that provide space for songwriting, creative thinking, improvisation, music production, individuality, and autonomy are central identifiers of its relevance in formal learning contexts (Cremata, 2017, 2019). This raises important questions about *how* instructors teach, facilitate, and coach meaningful music experiences in commercial and popular music settings – questions that may guide our thinking and offer insights into the future direction of teaching and learning commercial and popular music in higher education (Kladder, 2020).

A New Direction: Considering Popular and Commercial Music in Higher Education

The future of studying and experiencing music in higher education is bright if we collectively work together to realize the challenges ahead of us and if we take action to change what needs to be changed. The integration of commercial and popular music does not mean that all other music – the music we have been teaching for over a hundred years in the US – will disappear. It simply means we need to do more than most of us currently are doing. Regardless of the barriers that exist when integrating commercial and popular music in higher education, it is imperative that – as a profession – we acknowledge the need to further expand music offerings. We also may need to diversify our pedagogy, recognize weaknesses in teacher-directed models, and learn about more relevant and meaningful approaches for music learning in contemporary culture. The purpose of this book is to provide needed guidance, ideas, and support for faculty interested in exploring new notions of musicianship and pedagogy in higher education. Specifically, this book is intended for faculty who want to expand musicianship experiences in the commercial and popular music medium in ways that support a concerted effort to break down barriers of access for potential students who are interested in studying music in higher education. Each author in this book offers insights into how each specific context – all integrated from a commercial and popular music perspective – can support a more diverse, equitable, and inclusive music experience for students in higher education.

References

Birkett, J. (1992). Popular music education-the dawning of a New Age. *Popular Musicology*, *11*(2), 239–241.

Byo, J. L. (2018). "Modern Band" as school music: A case study. *International Journal of Music Education*, *36*(2), 259–269.

Cavicchi, D. (2009). My music, their music, and the irrelevance of music education. In Thomas A. Regelski, J. Terry Gates (Eds.), *Music education for changing times* (pp. 97–107). Dordrecht: Springer.

Cremata, R. (2017). Facilitation in popular music education. *Journal of Popular Music Education*, *1*(1), 63–82.

Cremata, R. (2019). Popular music: Benefits and challenges of schoolification. In Z Moir, B Powell, GD Smith (Eds.), *The Bloomsbury handbook of popular music education: Perspectives and practices* (p. 415). New York, NY.

Cutietta, R. A. (1991). Popular music an ongoing challenge. *Music Educators Journal*, *77*(8), 26–29.

Davis, S. G., & Blair, D. V. (2011). Popular music in American teacher education: A glimpse into a secondary methods course. *International Journal of Music Education*, *29*(2), 124–140.

Dyndahl, P., Karlsen, S., Nielsen, S. G., & Skårberg, O. (2017). The academisation of popular music in higher music education: The case of Norway. *Music Education Research*, *19*(4), 438–454.

Green, L. (2002). *How popular musicians learn: A way ahead for music education.* Surrey, England: Ashgate Publishing, Ltd.

Holley, S. (2021). Popular music programs – US. https://steveholleymusic.com/popular-music-programs-united-states. Accessed June 11, 2021.

Jaffurs, S. E. (2004). The impact of informal music learning practices in the classroom, or how I learned how to teach from a garage band. *International Journal of Music Education*, *22*(3), 189–200.

Kladder, J. (2020). Re-envisioning music teacher education: An investigation into curricular change at two undergraduate music education programs in the US. *Arts Education Policy Review*, *121*(4), 141–159.

Kladder, J. (2021). An autoethnography of a punk rocker turned music teacher. *Research and Issues in Music Education, 16*(1), 4.

Koza, J. E. (2009). Listening for whiteness: Hearing racial politics in undergraduate school music. In TA Regelski, JT Gates (Eds.), *Music education for changing times* (pp. 85–95). Dordrecht: Springer.

Krikun, A. (2008). Popular music and jazz in the American junior college music curriculum during the Swing Era (1935–1945). *Journal of Historical Research in Music Education, 30*(1), 39–49.

Krikun, A. (2017). Teaching the 'people's music' at the 'people's college': Popular music education in the junior college curriculum in Los Angeles, 1924–55. *Journal of Popular Music Education, 1*(2), 151–164.

Little Kids Rock. (2021). *Modern band*. https://www.littlekidsrock.org/the-program/modernband/.

LoVetri, J. L., & Weekly, E. M. (2003). Contemporary commercial music (CCM) survey: Who's teaching what in nonclassical music. *Journal of Voice, 17*(2), 207–215.

Mantie, R. (2013). A comparison of "popular music pedagogy" discourses. *Journal of Research in Music Education, 61*(3), 334–352.

McIntyre, P. (2008). Creativity and cultural production: A study of contemporary Western popular music songwriting, *Creativity research journal 20*(1), 40–52.

McIntyre, P. (2016). Songwriting as a creative system in action. In P. McIntyre, J. Fulton & E. Paton (Eds.), *The creative system in action: Understanding cultural production and practice* (pp. 47–59). Houndmills, Basingstoke, Hampshire [England]; New York: Palgrave Macmillan.

McIntyre, P. (2019). Taking creativity seriously: Developing as a researcher and teacher of songwriting. *Journal of Popular Music Education, 3*(1), 67–85.

Palmer, C. M. (2011). Challenges of access to post-secondary music education programs for people of color. *Visions of Research in Music Education, 18*, 1–22.

Parkinson, T., & Smith, G. D. (2015). Towards an epistemology of authenticity in higher popular music education. *Action, Criticism and Theory for Music Education, 14*(1), 93–127.

Powell, B., & Burstein, S. (2017). Popular music and modern band principles. In G. D. Smith, Z. Moir, M. Brennan, S. Rambarran, & P. Kirkman (Eds.), *The Routledge research companion to popular music education* (pp. 243–254). London: Routledge.

Powell, B., Krikun, A., & Pignato, J. M. (2015). "Something's Happening Here!": Popular music education in the United States. *IASPM Journal, 5*(1), 4–22.

Powell, B., Smith, G. D., West, C., & Kratus, J. (2019). Popular music education: A call to action. *Music Educators Journal, 106*(1), 21–24.

Randles, C. (2018). Modern band: A descriptive study of teacher perceptions. *Journal of Popular Music Education, 2*(3), 217–230.

Regelski, T. A., & Gates, J. T. (Eds.). (2009). *Music education for changing times: Guiding visions for practice (Vol. 7)*. Dortrecht; New York: Springer Science & Business Media.

Shuker, R. (2010). *Understanding Popular Music*. London: Routledge.

Smith, G. D. (2016). Popular music in higher education. In Ioulia Papageorgi and Graham Welch (Eds.), *Advanced musical performance: Investigations in higher education learning* (pp. 65–80). Farnham: Routledge.

Tobias, E. S. (2012). Hybrid spaces and hyphenated musicians: Secondary students' musical engagement in a songwriting and technology course. *Music Education Research, 14*(3), 329–346.

Welch, G., & Papageorgi, I. (Eds.). (2014). *Advanced musical performance: Investigations in higher education learning*. Farnham: Ashgate Publishing, Ltd.

Williams, D. A. (2015). The baby and the bathwater. *The College Music Symposium, 55.* http://dx.doi.org/10.18177/sym.2015.55.fr.10883.

Williams, D. A. (2019). *A different paradigm in music education: Re-examining the profession*. New York: Routledge.

Williams, D., & Randles, C. (2017). Navigating the space between spaces: Curricular change in music teacher education in the United States. In M. Brennan, Z. Moir, P. Kirkman, S. Rambarran, & G.D. Smith (Eds.), *Popular music education: Paradigms, practices, pedagogies, problems* (pp. 46–59). Farnham, Surrey, UK: Ashgate Publishing.

Zollo, P. (2003). *Songwriters on songwriting*. Cambridge, MA: Da Capo Press.

1 Constructivism

An Epistemology for Commercial and Popular Music in Higher Education

Jonathan R. Kladder and Jazzmone Sutton

An Epistemology and Theoretical Framework for Teaching Commercial and Popular Music in Higher Education

The integration of commercial and popular music in higher education has emerged as a force warranting critical examination and reflection. Although efforts to expand commercial and popular music in higher education have existed for quite some time, in recent years its emergence in academia suggests that the landscape of formal music learning in colleges and universities may be changing at an unprecedented pace (Krikun, 2008). Integrating an epistemology for coaching and facilitating commercial and popular music in higher education suggests a way for instructors to provide authentic and meaningful music learning experiences in the curriculum as students engage with songwriting, improvisation, music production, and digital tools, all situated within a curriculum that will ideally be flexible, learner-led, and autonomous.

As Cremata (2019) pointed out, there are challenges related to the acceptance of commercial and popular music in preservice music teacher education programs, including Eurocentric practices and limited access to the profession because of strict audition protocols and years of classical practice required before entrance to the profession. This belief is echoed by Scott (2011), who argued that many music teacher education programs remain focused on teacher-directed instruction that emphasizes Western European art canon designations. In contrast, we posit that the growth and continued emergence of music education in the US are reliant upon accepting and implementing commercial and popular music learning experiences in higher education and that its pedagogical practices should be grounded in constructivism. In this modus, the music education profession would

DOI: 10.4324/9781003216728-2

expand to include a wider breadth and depth of music making, and the curriculum would ideally be built upon active involvement, where learners engage with real-world performance opportunities and socially collaborate with one another in learner-led rehearsals. This would encourage critical thinking skills as students evaluated, analyzed, and synthesized music with their instructors (Shively, 2015; Wiggins, 2007).

The purpose of this chapter is to interrogate best practices for the teaching and learning of commercial and popular music in higher education. We also advocate and promote commercial and popular music's integration into the curriculum and suggest that constructivism, both as an epistemology and a theory of music learning, offers a pathway for relevant and meaningful music learning needed in the profession. This is especially true in commercial and popular music, as musicians in this modus require a skill set that is dependent upon creativity, individual poise, personal artistry, diverse musicianship skills, and entrepreneurial thinking (Gaunt & Papageori, 2012).

Let the Show Begin! Building the Foundation for Meaningful Music Learning

Broadly, constructivism is defined as both an epistemological view of learning (Duffy & Jonassen, 1992) and a "theory about knowledge and learning; it describes both what 'knowing' is and how one 'comes to know'" (Fosnot, 1995, p. 1). Although constructivism is not necessarily a theory for teaching *per se*, it offers an awareness of a process of learning that can radicalize current models of instruction that are teacher-directed: methods that are highly curricularized and methodical in their approach. These methodical and curricularized forms of teaching are often disconnected from real-world application and isolated from meaningful learning experiences. Conversely, constructivism "suggests taking a radically different approach to instruction from that used in most schools" (Fosnot, 1995, p. 3) and rejects the notion that:

> meaning can be passed on to learners via symbols and transmission [of facts], that learners can incorporate exact copies of teachers' understanding for their own use, that whole concepts can be broken into discrete subskills, and that concepts can be taught out of context.
>
> (p. 3)

Although music making is an experience that can traverse all cultures, often university and college music programs do not reflect the cultures that surround the institution's community – they are isolated from popular culture. To bridge this gap, constructivism can assist in centralizing student interest and knowledge so that instructors listen to students' concerns, personal musical desires, or long-term goals. In this modus, the barrier between formal and informal music making deliberately erodes and music learning spaces become open to diverse perspectives related to music learning and performance. *This is an intentional process*: the erosion of this barrier widens the pathway for students to be involved in the decision-making process, supports a more inclusive, diverse, and equitable learning space, and ideally, showcases the diversity of students in each setting. As the learning pathway increases in breadth and depth, the representation of students and their cultures has the potential to create a more diverse place for music learning in ways that represent a broader representation of music styles and genres from popular culture. In turn, the curriculum and pedagogy associated with music learning becomes reflective of students' interests (Bradley, 2007).

There are four main attributes that support *how* a constructivist approach toward teaching and learning is unique. First, constructivism acknowledges that learning is connected to students' real-world experiences (Fosnot, 1995; Steffe & Gale, 1995; Webster, 2011). Therefore, new knowledge is "what we can do in our experiential world, the successful ways of dealing with the objects we call physical and the successful ways of thinking" (p. 7). In this modus, learning is actively a part of the surrounding community and representative of society, including its diverse cultures. Formal learning is therefore not isolated to the institution. Second, the *adaptability* of knowledge is central to the process of understanding learning. As Steffe and Gale (1995) wrote, "knowledge is adaptive" (p. 7), and "one should think of knowledge as a kind of compendium of concepts and actions that one has found to be successful, given the purposes one had in mind" (p. 7). Therefore, knowledge is malleable and flexible depending on its "states of events of an external world" (p. 7) and what goals are determined by the learner. This contrasts with a teacher-directed classroom, where factual knowledge is often disconnected from application, and learning follows a rigid path predetermined by the teacher. Within the traditional educational setting, methodized curriculum materials are often driven by the educator and preclude students from influence or autonomy. The power structure that is formed and upheld in this approach is controlling. It remains focused on conformity, thus creating a perception of learning that extends only as far as the educator's perspective. This can create an environment of forced uniformity, homogeneousness, and discrimination which are all antithetical to creativity, autonomy, diversity, equity, and inclusion in music teaching and learning.

Third, learning is not a rigid process or preset understanding of what is needed. It is not method-driven or curricularized. Instead, learning is replaced with the "notion of viability" (p. 7). Simply understood, a constructivist approach recognizes that there is not one specific or identifiable truth and that the habits of mind, or particular epistemological views of how things *have* to be, are changed to reflect a malleable and adaptive, or flexible, design in learning. Therefore, learning is *active*. It requires that learners engage with the world in ways that break down the traditional conceptions of brick-and-mortar classrooms. In this modus, students participate and engage with their environment in real ways, actively explore their world, and absorb learning through hands-on and discovery-type approaches. As Steffe and Gale (1995) argued: "learning is not a stimulus-response phenomenon. It requires self-regulation and the building of conceptual structures through reflection and abstraction. Problems are not solved by the retrieval of rote-learned 'right' answers" (p. 14). Constructivism requires that learners identify their *own* problems through guidance from a teacher and then seek out approaches toward solving those problems.

Fourth, theorists define constructivism as a social and collaborative experience, meaning that when new knowledge is gained, it should regularly be thought of as a social activity where learners interact with one another in problem-solving, problem-finding, and action-engaged experiences. As Steffe and Gale (1995) argued, social interactions create a place where learners network with their world through lived experiences, explaining that "the 'others' with whom social interaction takes place are a part of the environment, no more but also no less than any of the relatively 'permanent' objects the child constructs within the range of his or her lived experience" (p. 12). Through collaboration with teachers and learners, students develop a sense of autonomy and ownership, which ideally will be sustainable over time. This sustained autonomy can be transferred to other musical learning experiences and offer possibilities for musical participation and creative music making across the lifespan.

The intentions of a constructivist approach are to create a learning environment where teachers and students work collaboratively within an equitable and diverse setting. Students are encouraged to develop decision-making skills and engage with one another in ways that foster critical thinking, including analysis, synthesis, and application (Hanna, 2007). Also, creative thinking is placed at the forefront of nearly every music learning decision. A constructivist epistemology privileges the knowledge students bring to the learning environment by utilizing it as a central part of the learning process as they become actively engaged in the decision-making process. Through the development of decision-making and critical thinking skills with guidance and facilitation from their instructors, a student's sense of autonomy and confidence increases. The combination of confidence and autonomy serve as internal support for students during points of struggle and success. These attributes are also evident in independent and group music making experiences. As the traditional power structure shifts from a teacher-dominated approach to one with more equal sharing of responsibilities, music educators and students become co-creators in the music making experiences and they learn from and teach one another. Shared power, responsibility, and learning are central tenets in the process. Achieving an environment that implements constructivism results in a sharing of power, responsibility, and learning, which will take time and certainly have its challenges.

Applying Constructivism to Commercial and Popular Music in Higher Education

The application of constructivism to music learning, and specifically to higher education in commercial and popular music contexts, is limited. In music broadly, the most notable contributions should be afforded to Webster (2011), who wrote that constructivism offers a process where:

> (1) knowledge is formed as part of the learner's active interaction with the world; (2) knowledge exists less as abstract entities outside the learner and absorbed by the learner; rather, it is constructed anew through action; (3) meaning is constructed with this knowledge; and (4) learning is, in large part, a social activity.
>
> (p. 36)

In popular music education, specifically in K-12 applications, Kladder (2020) argued that Little Kids Rock's Modern Band programs would ideally support a constructivist design, where creativity and songwriting are the locus of the students' learning process as they make the most of their musical decisions through social interactions with their peers. Kladder's (2020) considerations for teaching popular music are echoed by Cremata (2017, 2019), who suggested the benefits of a "guide-on-the-side" (p. 64) approach to music learning in ways that support socially constructed learning environments. Cremata (2019) also argued that method-driven approaches reduce opportunities for learners to experience and make music in meaningful, creative, and self-directed ways. Lebler (2008) also wrote about the importance of peer learning in popular and commercial music contexts, arguing that when students learn popular music, they should ideally teach each other and learn from one another in social contexts. These notions echo Green's (2002) considerations for how popular musicians learn and those studied by Burnard (2012, 2013) in the creative music making process.

These authors offered considerations for the profession that expose a similar theme: there is a danger in over-"methodizing" and over-"circularizing" music learning in this milieu. Regelski (2002) paralleled this argument, stating that music educators often push for clear, systematic, and assessment-driven methods, which are antithetical to the processes of learning suggested in this text. This is supported by Cremata (2019), who wrote that "hopefully the development of PME [popular music education] materials will not inspire legions of discipleship" (p.423), and that practitioners would "carefully unpack prepackaged curricula organized in preplanned lessons that require little in the way of teacher innovation, student/cultural considerations, and teacher supplemental planning" (p. 423). Others, including Scott (2006, 2011), wrote about the challenges facing the profession, where college and university courses embed teacher-directed pedagogy in course curricula and often strip music learning of its authenticity and culturally relevant experiences.

In higher education, and specifically in music teacher education, the acceptance and inclusion of commercial and popular music suggest a need to interrogate the types of pedagogy associated with musical learning in this medium. We can learn from our peers in the music industry. Ideally, we would resist the simplicity of creating method-driven and top-down instruction that is disconnected from real-world practice and culturally unresponsive to the diversity of potential students in the commercial and popular music medium. Change begins by transforming rehearsal spaces from teacher-directed to learner-led (Williams & Kladder, 2019). For example, in a digital controller ensemble, students would primarily lead the rehearsal: they would choose the music and repertoire they are interested in learning, with guidance from their coach. This automatically connects students' out-of-school music experiences to music learning within the institution. In the process of learning music, students would research the necessary elements they need to recreate or create music using online tools, collaboration with peers or instructors, or even musicians from outside the institution. For example, students would listen to chord progressions and rhythmic intricacies by ear to figure their parts out and source the software and tools they might need to perform these various soundscapes. This holds similarities to how popular musicians learn (Green, 2002). In this way, students would take ownership of their music learning. Finally, students might seek collaborative opportunities to create and share music with popular musicians from the local community, whereby they could write, arrange, and perform music with popular musicians outside the institution. This process connects students' lived experience within the institution to real-world applications outside it, as they perform "gigs" *with* other popular musicians beyond the college or university performance halls. In this modus, students take charge of their learning experiences and make musical decisions within an environment they have helped to create. They are guided through the process rather than being told what to do or how to do it.

These approaches hold particularly strong merit in an industry that is constantly changing and evolving, as musicians and producers are employed in a music industry that evolves quickly and relies on adaptability, collaboration, entrepreneurial thinking, creativity, problem-solving, and ingenuity. Connection to real-world performing musicians provides experiences for students to learn about and experience first-hand what it is like to work and perform in this type of industry. The successful integration of commercial and popular music in higher education would ideally build learning experiences using a constructivist epistemology, one where music learning is individualized, social, self-directed, collaborative, experimental, active, process-focused, and connected to real-world practice. It would celebrate diverse musicianships and be inclusive of a wide range of instruments and musical styles. In this modus, a diverse set of learners would establish relevant and meaningful musical goals with the facilitators (instructors) who could support them. Higher education would not – and should not – assume it can supply all the skills and knowledge needed for the 22nd-century musician but rather support the needs of students depending upon their career goals and provide all means to help reach them.

To visualize the aforementioned attributes for music learning in commercial and popular music milieu, a rhizomatic model is proposed. The model is represented as a rhizome because it suggests no central beginning or end to the learning process. Instead, learning occurs in a continuous rhizo-circular movement and transpires through social-collaborative networks. The rhizome embodies an anthropological metaphor – a nomadic lifestyle, one associated with constant movement, teamwork, and collaboration, where new knowledge is created by the development of innovative approaches and technological advances.

A rhizome suggests similar themes to a constructivist epistemology as well: a moving network of knowledge, co-created by students and faculty, who collaboratively design and redesign learning goals within a flexible and changing framework; a set of goals may include specific musical or non-musical attributes, using a self-directed and reflective approach, where learning is regularly connected to real-world practice in the music industry (Figure 1.1).

Challenges with Constructivist Approaches in Higher Education

Integrating an epistemology and theory of music learning in popular and commercial music that embraces constructivism will present its challenges. It may require a complete rethinking of the teaching process or music

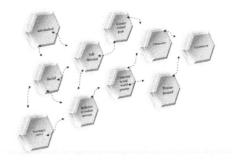

Figure 1.1 A rhizomatic model of constructivist learning for facilitating commercial music in music teacher education.

curricula, one where teachers "think like constructivists" (p. 192). In popular and commercial music, particularly in higher education, this can create challenges for instructors, who will be required to reinvent the way the classroom, applied studio, or ensemble context has historically existed. This can cause a disequilibrium for those new to the approach, as predetermined strategies for teaching are not the means for content to be integrated into the learning environment in a constructivist ensemble, classroom, or studio (Cremata, 2019).

When addressing issues of social justice in popular and commercial music, particularly in higher education, a constructivist approach relies on open discussions that are student-led so that facilitators listen and understand the level of musicianship, musical background, and personal experiences that have shaped their students' (and their personal) understandings of music. This openness, although important and valuable, might cause new challenges for facilitators, particularly those who have limited experience in dealing with complex social justice issues that exist in our society and culture. We may need further training on diversity and equity. We may need to read research related to breaking down racism in our society, culture, and, more specifically, in our profession. Emerging topics in higher education related to racism are at the forefront of the profession, and resources now abound. The time to embrace efforts to eliminate racism, specifically in music education, is now. It is incumbent on the instructor to listen and understand student voices, change the direction of a rehearsal, class, or studio lesson as needed, and integrate a holistic understanding of our students' musical and non-musical backgrounds.

The personality and ability of the instructor are also central factors when adopting constructivist approaches to music learning. In addition to the

constant reflective practices, implementing a constructivist
res strong interpersonal skills, as facilitators navigate a chal-
between student and teacher voice. As Scott (2011) wrote:

> the efficacy of this approach depends on the teachers' ability to see
> the road ahead: to offer direct instruction when students need specific
> content knowledge, and in dialogue with students, provide educational
> environments where students bring analytic awareness to music and the
> processes of music performance.
>
> (p. 192)

Kladder (2019) also wrote that a learner-led approach, one embedded in a
constructivist epistemology, relies on a constant recognition for pedagogy
to shift quickly across a continuum of learning. At times, an instructor will
guide music learning; at others, moments of direct instruction may be warranted. For example, in a pop/rock ensemble, the coach may need to teach
a particular scale pattern or mode for a particular song. In this modus, the
environment would shift quickly to a teacher-directed one, as the coach
teaches the scale pattern to each of the guitar or keyboard players. Once the
scale is learned, the space would shift swiftly back to a learner-led experience, as students integrate their new skills and lead the remaining portion of
the rehearsal. This ebb and flow will require constant flexibility, adaptation,
and open listening. As Ferm (2005) wrote:

> Sometimes the whole route is planned, and other times the area of
> activity is the only thing planned beforehand. A crossroad can be the
> ground for discussions, as well as direct decisions. Why teachers and
> pupils come to a crossroad can have different reasons. The teacher
> might decide the "right" way or offer several ones to choose from. The
> teacher's openness to the pupils as individuals and awareness about
> possible alternatives, are the basis for further experience.
>
> (p. 245)

Social and collaborative experiences require facilitators to be nimble and
quick, where initiated discussions require students to critically think and
analyze specific content. For some students, this may be a new experience, as much of music education relies on teacher-directed approaches
(Frazee, 2006; Scott, 2006, 2011; Webster, 2011). Changing the culture
in an ensemble, studio, or classroom may require time, persistence, and
slow integration. Although there is no utopian approach, constructivism
challenges us to think differently about music instruction. As a theoretical
framework, it offers suggestions that challenge us to think critically about

how music experiences are shaped and created so that music learning is learner-led and relevant.

That's a Wrap: Considerations for Change in Higher Education

The inclusion of commercial and popular music in higher education embedded in a constructivist epistemology for music learning may require a shift in pedagogical practices. As Scott (2011) wrote, "viewing curriculum development and implementation from constructivist perspectives requires reform" (p. 192), and he argued, "we must move away from purely teacher-directed centered instruction in which students are regarded as passive receptors of knowledge and toward student-centered approaches in which learners explore ideas related to their own insights" (p. 192). The emergence of popular and commercial music, when embedded in a constructivist design, offers one way to address issues of diversity, equity, and inclusion by providing relevant and emerging music making experiences deemed important and valuable for students in contemporary culture (Powell, Krikun, & Pignato, 2015).

As commercial and popular music proliferates throughout the educational landscape, faculty that guide preservice music teacher education programs in higher education will also need to expand, adapt, and integrate more commercial and popular music experiences in the curriculum. Creating new music learning opportunities for students interested in career pathways for teaching, marketing, or producing music in this medium will be necessary. This will mean expanding audition requirements, providing new method courses, and creating digital instrument studios and performance opportunities (Kladder, 2021). Furthermore, the shift toward a constructivist epistemology in support of learner-led approaches will require involvement from multiple stakeholders. As Scott (2011) wrote:

> To act as change agents, teacher educators need support. This can take many forms, including in-service opportunities to explore the implications of constructivist theories for learning, release time for revising current courses to reflect constructivist perspectives, or the development of new courses using these perspectives. The time required for these tasks needs to be valued within institutions of higher education.
> (p. 197)

Faculty will need to develop new curricula and work diligently to address exclusive, elitist, and inequitable practices in music teacher education, with purposeful intentions to expand notions of musicianship in ways that are accepting of popular and commercial music in higher education. However, as this chapter suggests, careful consideration of its intended purpose and goals is warranted.

In conclusion, we argue that adopting new pedagogical processes, ones that are antithetical to teacher-centered and method-driven instruction, are central to creating relevant and genuine commercial and popular music experiences in higher education. Including commercial and popular music in higher education offers *one* path toward expanding access and diversity in our institutions, but it is certainly not the only path. As each author illuminates in the following chapters of this book, there are direct connections between the pedagogical choices made in the classroom and meaningful music making experiences for students pursuing careers in music. Constructivism provides a framework to guide our thinking when developing new curricula in commercial and popular music education. Building a future of diverse learners and musicians in higher education relies on faculty who will take bold steps to confront the issues currently facing our profession. Let's work together to create new spaces for musicians that are equitable for all – particularly those from the commercial and popular music milieu – so they might learn in meaningful and relevant ways.

Reflection Questions

1. What changes can you make in your studio, ensemble, or classroom that support at least two of the guiding constructivist tenets outlined in this chapter?
2. What can you do at your institution to build a more equitable and inclusive learning environment within a constructivist epistemology?
3. How much are teacher-directed and method-driven approaches built into your curriculum, and how can you change this?
4. Have you, as the instructor, taken a "guide-on-the-side" approach, or do you remain the "sage on the stage" (Cremata, 2017, p. 64)? Why? How can this change?

References

Bradley, D. (2007). The sounds of silence: Talking race in music education. *Action, Criticism, and Theory for Music Education, 6*(4), 132–162.

Burnard, P. (2012). *Musical creativities in practice*. London: Oxford University Press.

Burnard, P. (2013). *Developing creativities in higher music education: International perspectives and practices*. New York: Routledge.

Cremata, R. (2017). Facilitation in popular music education. *Journal of Popular Music Education, 1*(1), 63–82.

Cremata, R. (2019). Popular music: Benefits and challenges of Schoolification. In Z. Moir, B. Powell & G. D. Smith (Eds.), *The Bloomsbury handbook of popular music education: Perspectives and practices* (pp. 415–428). London.

Duffy, T. M., & Jonassen, D. H. (1992). Constructivism: New implications for instructional technology. In T. M. Duffy & D. H. Jonassen (Eds.), *Constructivism and the technology of instruction: A conversation* (pp. 1–16). Hillsdale, NJ: Lawrence Erlbaum.

Ferm, C. (2005). Openness and awareness—Roles and demands of music teachers. *Music Education Research, 8*(2), 237–250.

Fosnot, C. T. (1995). *Constructivism: A psychological theory of learning. Theory, perspectives and practice.* New York: Teachers College Press.

Frazee, J. (2006). *Orff Schulwerk today: Nurturing musical expression and understanding.* New York: Schott Music.

Gaunt, H., & Papageorgi, I. (2012). Music in universities and conservatories. In S. Hallam & A. Creech (Eds.), *Music education in the 21st century in the United Kingdom: Achievement, analysis and aspirations* (pp. 260–278). London: The Institute of Education, University of London.

Green, L. (2002). *How popular musicians learn: A way ahead for music education.* Aldershot: Ashgate Publishing, Ltd.

Hanna, W. (2007). The new Bloom's taxonomy: Implications for music education. *Arts Education Policy Review, 108*(4), 7–16.

Kladder, J. (2019). Learner-centered teaching: Alternatives to the established norm. In D. A. Williams & J. R. Kladder (Eds.), *The learner-centered music classroom: Models and possibilities* (pp. 1–17). New York: Routledge.

Kladder, J. (2020). Re-envisioning music teacher education: An investigation into curricular change at two undergraduate music education programs in the US. *Arts Education Policy Review, 121*(4), 141–159.

Kladder, J. (2021). An autoethnography of a punk rocker turned music teacher. *Research and Issues in Music Education, 16*(1), 4.

Krikun, A. (2008). Popular music and jazz in the American junior college music curriculum during the Swing Era (1935–1945). *Journal of Historical Research in Music Education, 30*(1), 39–49.

Lebler, D. (2008). Popular music pedagogy: Peer learning in practice. *Music Education Research, 10*(2), 193–213.

Powell, B., Krikun, A., & Pignato, J. M. (2015). "Something's Happening Here!": Popular music education in the United States. *IASPM Journal, 5*(1), 4–22.

Regelski, T. (2002). On "methodolatry" and music teaching as critical and reflective praxis. *Philosophy of Music Education Review, 10*(2), 102–123.

Scott, S. (2006). A constructivist view of music education: Perspectives for deep learning. *General Music Today, 19*(2), 17–21.

Scott, S. (2011). Contemplating a constructivist stance for active learning within music education. *Arts Education Policy Review, 112*(4), 191–198.

Shively, J. (2015). Constructivism in music education. *Arts Education Policy Review, 116*(3), 128–136.

Steffe, L. P., & Gale, J. E. (Eds.). (1995). *Constructivism in education.* New York: Psychology Press.

Webster, P. R. (2011). Construction of music learning. In R. Colwell & P. R. Webster (Eds.), *MENC handbook of research on music learning: Volume 1* (pp. 35–83). New York: Oxford University Press.

Wiggins, J. (2007). Authentic practice and process in music teacher education. *Music Educators Journal, 93*(3), 36–42.

Williams, D. A., & Kladder, J. R. (2019). *The learner-centered music classroom: Models and possibilities*. New York: Routledge.

2 From Tin Pan Alley to Trending

Remixing Ragtime and South Asian Popular Music with Digital Audio Workstations

Adam patrick bell and Oshadhee Satarasinghe

Introduction

In this chapter, we provide readers with three sequential activities to teach digital audio workstation (DAW) skills adhering to a constructivist approach. DAW skills are elemental to contemporary music making practices (Seabrook, 2015). This makes DAWs the main instrument of modern music production (Bell, 2018). Therefore, if learners want to make contemporary popular music, they need to develop DAW skills. Historically, DAW skills have been self-taught following a trial-and-error approach (Bell, 2018), but colleges and universities can enhance this mode of learning by providing the infrastructure (i.e., recording equipment) and expertise (i.e., experienced teachers) needed to facilitate learner-centered experiences. In this chapter, we highlight the works of Black and South Asian composers and songwriters to model an anti-racist pedagogical approach. DAWs reflect the priorities of their designers, which determine or guide musical possibilities and limitations (Bell, 2015). Most DAW designs have Western biases, which make them challenging to use to produce popular musics of non-Western cultures (Faber, 2021). Readings on the topic of decolonizing the DAW suggested by Silpayamanant (2021) can serve as prompts for learners to think further and critically about DAW curricular designs.

We commence with two activities that focus on popular music of the early 20th century, namely ragtime, and proceed with a discussion and activity centered on South Asian popular music. The first activities are designed to take up to an hour (one class), while the final activity will require an additional one-hour class. Our activities assume that the facilitator has experience with DAWs, but for readers who are new to this discipline, we suggest *Music Technology 101* (Jones, 2021) as a primer.

DOI: 10.4324/9781003216728-3

Context

The activities outlined in this chapter were designed for an undergraduate-level introductory music technology course at the University of Calgary, Canada. The course typically draws learners who have diverse musical interests and varied experiences working with music technologies and popular music. To accommodate such a broad range of interests and experiences in the classroom, a scaffolded approach that gives learners the agency to make their own musical choices is needed. Our activities are designed to support learners with a range of music technology skills. We strive to strike a balance between the challenge of each activity and each learner's level of skill and experience such that all involved can be engaged in meaningful music making. While we prioritize music making in these activities, we also attempt to provide some historical and cultural context to provide learners with a rationale for our activities.

Tin Pan Alley and the Player Piano

We begin the first activity with some background information on Tin Pan Alley, because it was the world's first hit factory and the birthplace of the commercial music industry (Seabrook, 2015). Its name is attributed to the clash of sounds emitted from the corpus of compact studios crammed into a few New York City blocks (28th and 29th Streets between 5th and 6th Avenues), but it is also a metonym for the music industry and the mode of music production that flourished in the early 20th century (Suisman, 2009, p. 21). Typically, a studio was merely a room with a piano in which a songwriter churned out new tunes in hopes of spawning a sellable song. Given that Tin Pan Alley was a competitive industry, some songwriters even went as far as muting their pianos by placing newspapers between the strings to prevent a nearby listener from stealing their earworm-in-progress (Meyer, 1958, p. 39).

For a passerby, the experience of walking through Tin Pan Alley was akin to being immersed in the din of clanging pots and pans. What distinguished Tin Pan Alley was its prizing of (sheet) music as a commodity to be bought and sold – a good song was measured quantitatively by its profitability, as opposed to being assessed qualitatively for its other values (Suisman, 2009, p. 22). As a result, songs were more assembled than written, following a tried-and-tested formula of ensuring that the title of a song was also the first line of its chorus, and the chorus was the most memorable part of the song, which was repeated frequently, so as to lodge the melody in the listener's memory (pp. 48–49). This led to the development of the piano roll. The piano roll itself is a perforated scroll of paper premised on two basic design concepts making it resemble a spreadsheet: (1) pitches from low to high are organized left to right on the scroll, and (2) note durations are organized from top to bottom, with longer notes associated with longer rows of perforations, and vice versa (see Figure 2.1).

It is easier to grasp how a player piano works by experiencing it rather than explaining it, so for a reference we suggest watching "Piano Roll Production at QRS Music" (www.youtube.com/watch?v=i3FTaGwfXPM), which outlines the following description of the mechanics of a player piano:

> Player pianos are vacuum operated. The piano roll is drawn past a tracker bar, which contains a small hole corresponding to each note on the piano. When a hole in the paper exposes a hole in the tracker bar, a small bellows pushes the corresponding note on the piano.
>
> (cc213t, 2007, 0:19)

Player pianos peaked in popularity in the first decade of the 20th century, but faded into obscurity by the 1930s as radio became the dominant medium for experiencing music (Suisman, 2009, p. 16). In its heyday, the player piano attracted the likes of Bartók, Mahler, Prokofiev, Rachmaninoff, Debussy, Ravel, Scriabin, Stravinsky, Gershwin, and Joplin (McBride, 2014). This list of composers evidences that the practice of recording music using the piano roll medium was predominantly the preserve of white men. Learners should be alerted to this fact and consider the societal conditions at this time that dictated access to this technology. Hyman (1998) suggests that George Gershwin was drawn to the player piano because it enabled what we now call overdubbing – adding more to the performance after it has already been recorded. Arguably, no one explored the compositional possibilities of the

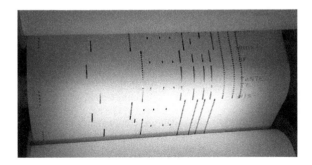

Figure 2.1 Using light to read piano rolls. Marty McGuire/Creative Commons/CC by 2.0 https://creativecommons.org/licenses/by/2.0/

player piano more than Mexican composer Conlon Nancarrow, who in the mid-20th century composed 49 studies specifically for the player piano. In these studies, Nancarrow crafted compositions that were unplayable for humans as they took advantage of the fact that a player piano could play more notes simultaneously (40) and faster (200/second), resulting in poly-everything pieces (e.g., rhythm, tempo, meter) (Hocker, 2002). Conlon's studies for player piano are easily accessible on YouTube, and we suggest "Study 37" as an example to share with learners.

Today, player piano rolls are relatively inexpensive and can be purchased new from QRS (www.qrsmusic.com/) for $15 or secondhand from reseller sites such as eBay for less than $5. We have found piano rolls to be a worthwhile teaching tool because learners report that examining the tangible medium is helpful in understanding how it works. It may also be beneficial to introduce learners to mechanical music more broadly, of which there are a wealth of examples on YouTube (see Table 2.1).

Another valuable resource is Joe Rinaudo's YouTube channel, which features him playing an American Fotoplayer – a player piano with an added percussion section. Fotoplayers were played by one person in movie theatres to provide soundtracks in the era of silent film. These means of mechanical music serve as a reminder that people have been programming music for centuries and that computer-based music is built upon the same underlying principles.

The Piano Roll and MIDI

It is no coincidence that within most DAWs, the MIDI editor is commonly referred to as "the piano roll." The piano roll interface within a DAW is a prime example of "skeuomorphism" (Bell et al., 2015), a design reference from a preceding technology that is not necessary for

Table 2.1 Piano roll examples for DAW activities

Artist	Song	Year	Link
A-ha	"Take On Me"	1985	www.youtube.com/watch?v=rbvY0VT3SJI
Queen	"Bohemian Rhapsody"	1975	www.youtube.com/watch?v=JTnGI6Knw5Q
Idina Menzel	"Let It Go" from *Frozen*	2015	www.youtube.com/watch?v=vwhv6EmkkKU
Dr. Dre	Medley	2017	www.youtube.com/watch?v=DpJtsktNcmc
Joe Rinaudo	Various	Present	www.youtube.com/channel/UCEWQTsDz39znxWbohaQPoKw

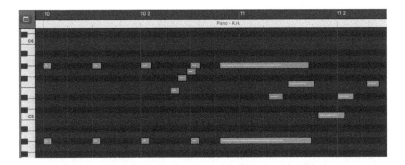

Figure 2.2 An example of a piano roll in a digital audio workstation platform.

functionality. However, the piano roll concept is intuitive and has been retained in most DAW designs. In the piano roll, users can create or edit the primary parameters of MIDI: note pitch, duration, and velocity (see Figure 2.2).

Making music with a blank piano roll can be approached by adding notes one-by-one using the pencil tool or the more common method of using a MIDI controller, such as piano keyboard, to record the performance in real time. For the purposes of familiarizing themselves with the piano roll, learners might commence with some ready-made materials. It has been our experience that learners prefer to start with something rather than with nothing. It is at this juncture that we can tap into Tin Pan Alley history and revive some piano rolls of yesteryear.

Fortunately, there exists a small group of archivist-appreciators of piano rolls that scan and convert them to MIDI files (.mid) without any cost. This constitutes a treasure trove of musical materials with which learners can engage. Furthermore, in the instances in which learners choose a roll that was performed by the composer (e.g., Joplin by Joplin), there is oftentimes an added element of appreciation due to the direct association. Because converting piano rolls to MIDI files is a niche activity, locating them can be a challenge. For example, at the time of writing, the website of one of the most prolific providers of scanned piano rolls – Warren Trachtman's trachtman.org – is not available. Although these sites are archaic-looking to many learners who have come of age in the current millennium, they offer much music ripe for remixing.

Activity 1: Recreating Tin Pan Alley

Piggybacking on our brief contextual introduction to Tin Pan Alley, which typically requires approximately 15 minutes, we proceed to our first music making activity called "Recreating Tin Pan Alley." The purpose of this short activity is to reconstruct the cacophony of Tin Pan Alley in a low-stakes atmosphere. We aim for learners to gain some familiarity with a DAW, particularly the piano roll, and have fun while doing so. Our rationale for beginning with this activity is that some learners find the task of creating music to be daunting and anxiety-inducing. While we have devised other strategies for easing learners into songwriting (see Bell, 2019), this first activity is designed to serve as a primer – a means of scaffolding learners to larger-scale projects. The activity can be facilitated in in-person classroom settings or completed remotely, but to get the immersive experience, it needs to be done synchronously. There are several different ways to begin this activity. We suggest the teacher attempt to steer learners' web searching to one of the following sites:

(1) Pianola: www.pianola.co.nz/public/index.php/wmidi/
(2) Kunstderfuge: www.kunstderfuge.com/piano-rolls.htm
(3) Terry Smythe: www.terrysmythe.ca/archive.htm
(4) The PrimeLime MIDI Library: www.primeshop.com/MIDILibrary/midlist2.htm

In this activity, we use the latter site, which has a dedicated page to African American composer Scott Joplin, who is best known for his ragtime pieces. We offer the following suggestions to facilitate this activity:

- **Step 1**: Encourage learners to explore the sites and audition rolls/files by different composers.
- **Step 2**: Be aware that learners who attempt to listen to .mid files directly as audio will discover it is not possible, which leads to an important concept they need to grasp: a MIDI file on its own cannot produce sound; rather, it is a set of instructions that a program processes to produce music.
- **Step 3**: There are many parameters that MIDI can control, but we focus on pitch, duration, and velocity (level). Depending on a given individual's device, what happens when they select a .mid file varies – the file may automatically open in the desired DAW as hoped, but alternatively, it may automatically open in a notation program, play on a media program, or do nothing at all.
- **Step 4**: Use the "Save as" approach so that learners download their files to a location of their choosing on their devices. Most DAWs provide a "drag and drop" and/or "import MIDI file" option. DAWs typically default to a piano sound setting, and learners should be able to listen to their imported MIDI files immediately.
- **Step 5**: Stage the first jaunt down Tin Pan Alley. For computer labs, have learners unplug their headphones and turn up their speakers. Provide a

countdown (e.g., "On the count of three, everyone press play"), and then give everyone an opportunity to stroll down mock Tin Pan Alley.

- **Note**: For online environments, the audio latency inherent in videoconferencing only adds to the charm of the desired Tin Pan Alley-esque chaos. In both in-person and remote scenarios, having everyone press play on their devices simultaneously shifts the focus away from the individual and onto the collective.

Activity 2: Ragtime Remix

After the first exercise is complete, we extend it to a second activity – "Ragtime Remix" – which requires 20 minutes. To foster a playful environment, our go-to strategy is adding a beat. In our demonstration to learners, we use Scott Joplin's "Maple Leaf Rag" (1899) and attempt to make a remix resembling boom bap-era hip hop. Here are the steps we follow:

- **Step 1**: Demonstrate for learners how they can quickly audition different sounds, such as shifting from a sine wave to a shakuhachi, using the same MIDI file.
- **Step 2**: While one sound may be sufficient, suggest to learners that they create a duplicate of the original MIDI track, but with a different sound. This then becomes an exercise in which learners can experiment with creating composite sounds, such as a harpsichord paired with a horn section or a kalimba accompanied by a koto.
- **Step 3**: Most DAWs have premade loops that can be added, or alternatively, learners can explore their DAW's beat-making possibilities. In our case, we use Logic's "Drummer" track feature and select "Maurice" as our pseudo-DJ Premiere playing an Music Production Centered (MPC).
- **Note**: Adding a beat can be truly transformative, and learners can decide for themselves whether "Maple Leaf Rag Boom Bap" is an achievement, an atrocity, or somewhere in between. More elements can be added, but in the interest of variety, we reserve these strategies for our third and final activity.

Activity 3: South Asian Remix

Activity 3 is designed as a follow-up activity and requires a one-hour class. Beyond piano rolls converted to MIDI files, there are numerous sources of free MIDI files on sites such as freemidi.org. While we define our starting point with Tin Pan Alley, we consciously choose not to define the moving target that is "trending" and instead leave it to learners to decide what other musical styles they want to engage with in this activity. We provide prompts to draw learners' attention to musics they may not have engaged with as much or at all. In this third activity, we focus on South Asian popular music. Many efforts have been made to help teachers select musics of diverse cultures thoughtfully (Abril, 2006), and design culture-specific and cross-cultural units (Abril, 2013). However, South Asian popular music is mostly absent in North American curricula. Sarazzin (2006) avers that South Asian music is underrepresented within school communities because of its lack of resources and instruments and unfamiliar language, timbres, and tonalities.

South Asian popular music mixes Indian traditional and Classical music, and Western techniques (Parimi, 2014). In the last decade, fusion between Indian and Western music has increased, especially among young North American-born South Asian musicians. Many of these musicians grew up having dual identities and not necessarily knowing how to integrate and combine Western and Indian musics. They learn Western music through schooling, and more broadly through American popular culture, while simultaneously learning Indian music in their homes and communities. Indo-Canadian musician Ghandi (not to be confused with Mahatma Gandhi) reflected: "Because I grew up in Canada, I feel like I have a unique perspective and many different musical influences that I'm now trying to combine in my music and represent someone who's not just Indian but also an Indo-Canadian" (Sciarpelletti, 2021).

Adding instrumentation to create fusion music is an emerging trend in the popular music world of Canadian, American, and British South Asian artists. Musicians such as Hithesh Sharma and Jay Sean have created distinctly South Asian sonic signatures within hip hop. Hithesh Sharma explained his approach of blending songs from his South Asian heritage with hip hop: "I just decided to load up a famous Bollywood song into my computer, chop it up and make a beat out of that!" (Sciarpelletti, 2021). For this activity, we provide some guiding ideas for how to incorporate South Asian popular music and thereby help foster a more culturally aware learning environment that represents South Asian people. Before commencing this activity, it is important to discuss with learners the differences between cultural appreciation and cultural appropriation in this context. Ultimately, learners will need to decide for themselves what is appropriate versus inappropriate, but the teacher should make a point to discuss potential ethical issues in cultural borrowing and the importance of engaging with culture bearers to inform and guide artistic decisions.

- **Step 1**: Explain how Indian and Western musics share some similarities, especially in melodic structures. Some similar scale structures include (1) the major pentatonic scale and Bhupali Raga, (2) Mixolydian (omit pitches 2 and 4) and Kalavathi Raga, (3) C Major and Bilawal Raga, and (4) Lydian and Kalyan Raga.

- **Step 2**: Emphasize that when incorporating a melodic instrument, it is important to find similar scale structures. Exemplars could include Jeffrey Iqbal & Purnash combining A.R. Rahman's "Tere Bina" (2006) with Maroon 5's "Girls Like You" (2017) (www.youtube.com/watch?v =Q3FEP6Uc2Hc), or Purnash combining Ben E. King's "Stand by Me" (1961) with "Kabhi Kabhi" (1976) as sung by Lata Mangeshkar and Mukesh (www.youtube.com/watch?v=96fkMw_LqGQ).
- **Step 3**: For demonstration purposes, we suggest fusing Ed Sheeran's "Thinking Out Loud" (2014) (www.mididb.com/ed-sheeran/thinking -out-loud-midi/) with A.R. Rahman's "Ishq Bina" from the film *Taal* (1999) (www.geocities.ws/kit_gautam/midi.html), both of which are available for free.
- **Note**: Compared to the MIDI files referenced in Activities 1 and 2 that typically consist of one or two tracks, more current MIDI files can consist of several instrument tracks.

We suggest that learners focus on the conventions of a given genre and how they can work with or against them to make something original. By this point, learners have already experimented with adding beats to ragtime, and we encourage the same strategy with South Asian popular music using a trial-and-error approach. In addition, we suggest the following strategies to increase complexity:

- Using premade loops is convenient but encourage learners to explore a DAW's beat-making instruments to experiment with the nuances of rhythm and timbre.
- Encourage learners to record beats in real time using a MIDI controller if they have access to one, or alternatively, use their QWERTY keyboard.
- Recording real-time performances opens a space to discuss rhythmic quantization, which is a means to align (or purposefully misalign) a rhythm in relation to the tempo.
- Understandably, learners new to quantizing tend to marvel at the instant fix it can provide, but we suggest a teaching moment involving J Dilla, known for disregarding quantization altogether. See, for example, "How J Dilla humanized his MPC3000" (www.youtube.com /watch?v=SENzTt3ftiU) (Vox, 2017).
- Beyond beats, instrumentation is a rich area to explore. DAWs often have some South Asian instruments, but if not, there are many websites that sell South Asian vocal samples (www.noiiz.com/sounds/ packs/1408), loops (www.soundsnap.com/tags/punjabi), and instruments (www.loopmasters.com/genres/147-India/products/559-Indian -Emotions).

- Depending on how many instrumental tracks a MIDI file contains, learners should consider whether they want to pursue an additive or subtractive strategy.
- Muting tracks can be an effective means to create a new arrangement, such as paring down to just drums and bass, a practice used in Jamaican dub production (Veal, 2007).
- Conversely, adding tracks such as a bass line or perhaps even vocals may be desirable.
- Recording vocals requires the introduction of audio, which is not the focus of these activities, but if learners are inclined to rap or sing, teachers can give an over-the-shoulder crash course on recording audio.
- Many DAWs can convert audio to MIDI, and this may be worth demonstrating, or at least mentioning to learners, as it may open up a new avenue with which to create MIDI tracks.
- Suggest exploring automation if the learner's DAW provides it. Automating simply means programming a parameter's behavior, such as having the volume of a track go up and down to create dynamism. Most parameters of an instrument or effect can be automated as well as performed with a MIDI controller such as a knob or slider on a keyboard.
- While it may be overwhelming to introduce effects in a primer activity, there are low-barrier approaches to exploring them, such as "FX Roulette" (Bell, 2020), that could be incorporated into this activity.

Ultimately, the learning context will determine the pacing of the activities and the time available to do them. The Tin Pan Alley approach to listening can be repeated if warranted, but given that more time and energy will have been invested into Activity 3, learners may request their remixes receive a focused listen. One strategy that eases learners into having everyone else listen to their music is to use a relay approach. Instead of having one person play their entire song and then receive feedback, then repeating the cycle, have everyone play an excerpt of their song (e.g., 30 seconds) and then "tag" the next person to play their excerpt without any discussion in between. This way, an entire group can share a part of their work in the span of minutes. Afterward, the teacher can facilitate a discussion about the accomplishments of the group.

Conclusion

Our activities combine technological and cultural history with contemporary commercial music practices and their associated skills. We are mindful that the needs and demands of a given teaching and learning context can significantly alter what is feasible and suitable. For these reasons, we encourage teachers to modify our approaches as appropriate. We suggest that DAW skills are fundamental to creating contemporary and popular music experiences and that the best way to learn these skills is to engage in the type of constructivist activities we have outlined in this chapter. By creating a context in which learners make their own musical choices yet have the guidance of a teacher to provide scaffolded prompts, DAW skills are learned authentically and can be honed through further experiences. Ultimately, the onus is on the teacher to ensure that learners experience low barriers to entry and can thrive to continually reach new heights in the domain of contemporary music production. Finally, DAWs provide a means by which learners can explore and engage with a broad range of musical cultures. In a learner-centered approach such as ours, we leave it to the learners to decide, but it is crucial for the teacher to lead by example and expand learners' musical horizons in this regard.

Reflection Questions

1. Do you agree with the statement that DAWs "should be considered core to music studies in learner-centered higher education"? Why or why not?
2. How has popular music and its production processes changed and/or stayed the same since the Tin Pan Alley era?
3. How does programming music, such as with a player piano or DAW, challenge and/or confirm your institution's explicit and implicit framing of musicianship? Consider: can/should students be admitted into an undergraduate program based on their DAW skills? Why or why not?
4. This chapter discusses popular music separated by more than a century. What other genres/styles that fall between 1900 and now are ripe for remixing?
5. Like South Asian popular music, what other cultures' popular musics are underrepresented in undergraduate music curricula? How can they be included such that these cultural practices are honored in non-tokenistic ways?

References

Abril, C. R. (2006). Music that represents culture: Selecting music with integrity. *Music Educators Journal*, *93*(1), 38–45.

Abril, C. R. (2013). Toward a more culturally responsive general music classroom. *General Music Today*, *27*(1), 6–11.

Bell, A. P. (2015). Can we afford these affordances? GarageBand and the double-edged sword of the digital audio workstation. *Action, Criticism, and Theory for Music Education, 14*(1), 44–65.

Bell, A. P. (2018). *Dawn of the DAW. The studio as musical instrument.* New York, NY: Oxford University Press.

Bell, A. P. (2019). Of trackers and top-liners: Learning producing and producing learning. In Z. Moir, B. Powell & G. D. Smith (Eds.), *The Bloomsbury handbook of popular music education* (pp. 171–185). London, UK; New York, NY: Bloomsbury.

Bell, A. P. (2020). FX roulette. In A. P. Bell (Ed.), *The music technology cookbook: Ready-made recipes for the classroom* (pp. 245–252). Oxford University Press.

Bell, A. P., Hein, E., & Ratcliffe, J. (2015). Beyond skeuomorphism: The evolution of music production software user interface metaphors. *Journal on the Art of Record Production.* https://www.arpjournal.com/asarpwp/beyond-skeuomorphism-the-evolution-of-music-production-software-user-interface-metaphors-2/.

cc213t. (2007, March 18). *Piano roll production at QRS music* [Video]. YouTube. https://www.youtube.com/watch?v=i3FTaGwfXPM.

Faber, T. (2021, February 25). Decolonizing electronic music starts with its software. *Pitchfork.* https://pitchfork.com/thepitch/decolonizing-electronic-music-starts-with-its-software/.

Hocker, J. (2002). My soul is in the machine — Conlon Nancarrow — Composer for player piano — Precursor of computer music. In H. Braun (Ed.), *Music and technology in the twentieth century* (pp. 84–96). Baltimore: The Johns Hopkins University Press.

Hyman, D. (1998, December). Rhapsody for George: A centennial celebration of Gershwin's legacy. *JAZZIZ,* 52–54.

Jones, H. (2021). *Music technology 101: The basics of music production in the technology lab or home studio.* Milwaukee, WI: Hal Leonard.

McBride, J. (2014, September 18). Introducing the Denis Condon collection of reproducing pianos and rolls. *Stanford University Libraries.* https://library.stanford.edu/blogs/stanford-libraries-blog/2014/09/introducing-denis-condon-collection-reproducing-pianos-and.

Meyer, H. (1958). *The gold in Tin Pan Alley.* Philadelphia, Lippincott: Greenwood Press.

Parimi, M. (2014). Musical mixes of 'classical' India and the West: Exploring novel styles [Honors research project, University of Redlands]. http://inspire.redlands.edu/alura/9/.

Sarrazin, N. (2006). India's music: Popular film songs in the classroom. *Music Educators Journal, 93*(1), 26–32.

Sciarpelletti, L. (2021, March 7). *From prairies to Bollywood: Record deal shows power of TikTok to get diverse artists noticed.* CBC. https://www.cbc.ca/news/canada/saskatchewan/hitesh-tesher-sharma-viral-tiktok-song-young-shahrukh-1.5878975.

Seabrook, J. (2015). *The song machine: Inside the hit factory.* New York: W.W. Norton & Company, Norton.

Silpayamanant, J. (2021, August 8). DAW, music production, and colonialism, a bibliography. *Mae Mai.* https://silpayamanant.wordpress.com/bibliography/daw -colonialism/.

Suisman, D. (2009). *Selling sounds: The commercial revolution in American music.* Cambridge, Mass: Harvard University Press.

Veal, M. E. (2007). *Dub: Soundscapes and shattered songs in Jamaican reggae.* Middletown, Connecticut: Wesleyan University Press.

Vox. (2017, December 6). *How J Dilla humanized his MPC3000* [Video]. Youtube. https://www.youtube.com/watch?v=SENzTt3ftiU.

3 The Electronic Digital Instrument

What Does It Mean to Develop Musical Skill with a Computer?

Michael Bierylo

Overview

The computer plays an important role in all aspects of contemporary musical life, and while all musicians use music technology to produce music, music creation and performance are increasingly focused on the computer (Keith, 2010). We see that emerging styles and genres are based on virtual electronic instruments and increasingly come from the imagination of producers. The term "producer" has greatly expanded over the history of contemporary music, and can now imply that one person, the *producer*, takes on the role of songwriter, composer, arranger, sound designer, and audio engineer. All the work in this modus revolves around the use of the computer. Where music creation has historically been centered on the piano, we are now seeing the computer as the point of focus. The computer is the piano of the 21st century. Given this undeniable truth, we need to reimagine how we teach music to reflect contemporary practice in higher education.

A traditional music curriculum is built on the idea that one learns music by playing it, but what we are currently seeing is people learning music by producing it (Tobias, 2013). Many young musicians with no formal training develop musical ideas by producing them. This may include other instruments or vocals, but by and large, many producers depend on pre-made samples, loops, and other assets and arrange them on a timeline. Electronic music producers often draw and edit MIDI notes instead of playing individual parts.[1] As a result, these musicians develop an acuity for developing musical ideas in the production process. What they lack in traditional musical training, they make up for with the ability to listen and analyze musical models from the industry and develop new ideas based on what they hear. This type of ear training guides their musical choices, and over time they can develop a sense of key with melodic and harmonic relationships. The first thing a producer will often learn is how to recognize and reproduce rhythmic patterns that define electronic music genres and use these skills to

DOI: 10.4324/9781003216728-4

make "beats" or "instrumental beds" that serve as the foundation for contemporary pop music. From here, fully formed songs in a variety of genres develop.

Developing musicians often have a desire to express themselves by playing music and inevitably find their way to a myriad of opportunities through traditional ensembles, such as bands, orchestras, and choirs offered through school programs. Sometimes they perform in less formal neighborhood garage bands. These opportunities have historically been the incubators for musical skill. Producers, on the other hand, find significant outlets for their musical work through social media, streaming platforms, and alternative methods of distribution. For those who want to get their music in front of a live audience, DJ sets are an important outlet. For many, this is their only performance experience. While these students may not have the musicianship skills of more traditionally trained musicians, they often have a good sense of what an audience wants or expects and work with larger musical forms, putting together sets that include a mix of different songs as their means of expression. Both online outlets and DJ performances produce revenue streams for electronic musicians at all levels, and early success here often leads to professional aspirations. These student producers often feel that the next step to achieving their goals is further study in college. A lack of traditional training, however, has kept these types of students out of collegiate music programs. Students auditioning to enter Berklee College of Music who are DJs or producers often remark that they have been unsuccessful at finding educational opportunities because they lack formal training on a traditional instrument.

Context and Background

As music educators, we are faced with the challenge of meeting the needs of young musicians who come from these types of alternative musical backgrounds. This challenge is not unique, and historically, the rise of jazz as a musical art form presented challenges to more traditional music education in the mid-20th century. At Berklee College of Music, one of our founding principles is that "musicianship could be taught through the music of the time" (Berklee College of Music, n.d.).[2] Because "music of the time" is in constant flux, Berklee is faced with the ongoing challenge of reconciling a comprehensive music education with the realities of contemporary music making. As music technology, and specifically the computer, has become a central part of music making, meeting the needs of students who come to music through production requires that we challenge the basic assumptions regarding pedagogy. One could make the case that musical skills could be taught through production, and in fact, this may be where music education is headed, but given a focus on instrumental skills in the Berklee curriculum, we chose to develop a program of study around the computer as the central part of a musical instrument. In doing so, we chose to use musical performance, and not production, as the point of reference for developing a curriculum.

While some student producers can start building careers or at least get paid from various sources, there are those who want a more formal music education. While the initial impetus for developing the program at Berklee was to attract students who are already electronic performers, the pool of applicants we see is mainly made up of producers, DJs, and singer-songwriters who use a computer to accompany themselves in a performance. Although we expect this to evolve as more students become aware of electronic performance possibilities, this is where we are now, and the program at Berklee offers non-traditional musicians the opportunity to take advantage of a contemporary music program, developing performance skills that build from prior experience as a fledgling producer. What follows is a case study of how Berklee has developed an electronic digital instrument (EDI) program, sharing our observations, pedagogical practices, and strategies. This is definitely a work in progress, and we look forward to adapting to the changing technology and student profile as our program grows.

The Electronic Digital Instrument at Berklee College of Music

The Beginning: Imaging a New Program

In imaging how a computer-based instrument could be defined, we wanted a very general description to encourage the greatest range of practitioners to apply and then inspire them to expand the range of techniques and devices used in their performance practice while studying music at Berklee. We have seen musicians explore the gamut of electronic, digital, and electro-acoustic possibilities and use them in live performances. This includes computers, mobile devices, MIDI controllers, digital and analog hardware synthesizers, modular synthesizers, turntables, drum machines, and sequencers, along with a nearly infinite array of effect devices. While the pedigree of all these devices is electronic, we see examples of sound generated through analog and digital means, and although the control of electronic sound is most often digital, we also see examples of performers using voltage control, most often with a modular synthesizer. Although the laptop computer seems central to many of these performance configurations, and it may be convenient to call the laptop a musical instrument, that is not entirely accurate. We have often heard the term "digital instrument," but this skirts the issue of analog devices used in a performance system. It might be tempting to call the laptop a musical instrument, but thinking of this general-purpose appliance as an instrument unto itself is indeed limiting. We feel the term "electronic digital instrument" is perhaps the most accurate way to categorize the broad range of devices that make up an electronic performance system that we call an instrument.

In acknowledging that this instrument is indeed a system, we defined the electronic digital instrument as a minimum configuration made up of a computing device with user-configured software and at least one performance controller. From this perspective, a mobile device such as a tablet or a phone could be considered an EDI. However, we most often see students using a laptop computer running software such as Ableton Live and at least one commonly available hardware controller forming the core of their performance system. While our model stresses real-time performance, we also need to consider the intelligence built into these systems as well as the ability to control pre-recorded material as part of the pedagogy. These capabilities are certainly a big part of what we mean when we designate an instrument as digital.

In planning for the EDI program at Berklee, we considered proposing a pilot program where students admitted with EDIs as their principal instruments would take their music core studies in a cohort with others, working through the curriculum together, using the computer and related controller in their studies.[3] Ultimately, we felt that isolating a group of students in a school with an overall enrollment of around 4,000 would deprive them of many of the opportunities afforded all other students at Berklee. Students attending Berklee with an EDI as their principal instrument take all the same core music classes as other music students, including theory, harmony, and ear training, and while some of their ensemble experience will be with purely EDI ensembles, our goal for these students is that they will be fully integrated with musicians using all types of instruments.[4] Students who play traditional instruments are often curious about their classmates who are EDI players, and we are seeing that challenge them when having to explain their chosen instrumental path. In the Spring 2018 commencement concert honoring Nile Rogers, among others, we saw a member of the EDI ensemble in a featured role performing using Ableton Live with a Push 2 controller, and from there we are seeing EDIs playing a visible role in contemporary popular music concerts produced by the college.

The Audition

Everyone who applies to Berklee goes through an audition and interview process. Assessing the skill of traditional instrumentalists is based on long-established norms for instrumental proficiency that guide the ratings of each student. EDI players are assessed using the same criteria as other instrumentalists. We require a prepared piece, sight reading, pitch, rhythm, and chordal recognition, as well as some form of improvisation. They demonstrate core musicianship skills by singing or playing back pitches and melodic phrases, clapping or playing back rhythmic examples, and identifying chord types by ear. These skills are assessed in the same way for any instrumentalist, but for self-taught musicians, these are valuable ways to predict a student's chance of success in a music program. While most students auditioning as EDI players are poor at sight reading, we feel that their ability to demonstrate core musical skills is an indicator of success in music studies at Berklee. Given that many students auditioning as EDI players lack traditional performance opportunities, we assess their prepared piece based on their potential for growth as a player. Sight reading is only one of the ratings in an audition. Students who score low can have that offset by strengths in other areas. This is sometimes the case with singers and other non-traditional instrumentalists as well. We see some very talented singers who perhaps learned music in church choirs but are weak sight readers. These students develop reading skills in the core music program.

The first challenge we faced in preparing for auditions was communicating expectations. While students coming from traditional music programs often learn what is expected in an instrumental audition from their private instructor or music director/conductor, EDI players are self-taught with little or no connection to school music programs. Although EDI musicians are experienced in using a DAW in music production, most of them have never considered how to use it in performance. In many cases, they have never performed in front of an audience outside of playing their tracks for others or DJing at local events. In addition, some DAWs that students use to produce music are not well suited for live performance, and students using those in an audition are often handicapped by their lack of performance capabilities. While some software functions students already use in music production, such as transport control, mix control, clip launching, and control of synthesizer and effect parameters, may be adapted to live performance, some students who want to audition as EDI principals at Berklee have never used them in the context of a performance. Those who use integrated hardware controllers are at a distinct advantage here, and the ability to navigate a performance without touching the laptop is one of the clearest indicators of one's aptitude for live electronic performance.

A common misconception that prospective EDI students often have is that we are mainly interested in their production skills, so they think that playing a track they have produced will work as their prepared piece. In preparing students to audition for the EDI program, an important goal was to clarify our expectations for what they would need to demonstrate in their prepared piece. The Berklee Office of Admissions offers specific guidelines to help students prepare for an EDI audition, including a video that demonstrates some of the techniques and skills they could demonstrate. In developing guidelines, our informal mantra was "Don't just press 'play' – *play*." While there are many possible modes of electronic performance, we chose to demonstrate live looping, loop variation, live effects processing, finger drumming, and live synthesizer playing in the video. We felt that these options would be some of the most obvious strategies students could use to translate a production into a live performance. Some elements of the performance would invariably be played as linear audio tracks, but we were looking for ways students could demonstrate real-time performance capabilities in ways that made it clear that they understood what it means to perform electronic music and that we could make an informed assessment of their overall skill and potential for the program.

EDI students are given reading examples that cover melodic phrases, bass parts, chord parts written in standard notation and chord symbols, as well as rhythmic notation. Examples are organized by rhythmic complexity, with melody, bass, and rhythm parts starting with simple duple rhythms moving to syncopated eighth and sixteenth notes. Students with prior musical training are generally the most successful in this part of the audition, and the variety of examples plays to the strengths of those with some prior formal training on keyboards or drums. We want to provide students with the opportunity to demonstrate that they can read music regardless of their prior musical training.

The final component of the audition is the prepared piece. In this portion of the audition, we can assess a student's prior commitment to performing electronic music. While the video we produced to clarify the process to prospective students demonstrates some electronic performance techniques, students are free to use any combination of hardware and software. We are looking for several key indicators: the ability to (1) play musical parts using some kind of controller, typically a keyboard or grid controller, (2) manipulate form during the performance, switching from one section to the next, (3) control effect processing and synthesizer parameters in real time, and (4) perform without needing to look at the computer or use key commands, a trackpad or mouse. As with any other performance, the ability to play and execute all controls in time is an important factor, as well as the overall mix and balance.

In order to facilitate a smooth audition process, special care needs to be taken in preparing the room. As a purely electronic instrument, students are totally dependent on the playback system for a successful audition. Much as we provide guitar and bass amps and drums for other auditions, a dependable, full-range stereo sound system is essential. An electronic performance will often depend on low frequencies, so having a system with a sub-woofer is ideal. Although we can provide an audio interface, we encourage students to bring their own. We provide all cables a student might need to connect to the sound system, including adapters for students who choose to use the audio output on their laptop. There is only stereo playback in the room, with no separate monitor system for vocals. In most cases, prospective students who use an instrument or vocals will connect to their audio interface and provide a stereo mix of all elements.

A team of two Berklee faculty members audition each student. While faculty are trained to evaluate musicians on a range of instruments, the EDI audition presents a unique challenge. The first and most obvious requirement is that a faculty member buy into the notion that the EDI is a musical instrument. In a school of contemporary music, this is often not an issue, as many of our faculty members are open and curious as to the possibilities of this way of performing. However, for the audition to be a fair and accurate assessment, one of the faculty members on the audition team needs to be well versed in electronic performance. We do not use a rubric for the evaluation but assign a rating of 1–8 with qualitative comments for each component of the audition. The audition process is a learning experience for all faculty, and as more faculty become involved in EDI auditions, we will need to develop a general rubric for evaluating skills specific to EDI.

The Electronic Digital Instrument Program

Overview

The EDI Principal Instrument program is part of the core music experience at Berklee. Core music studies require 41 credits toward a 120-credit Bachelor of Music degree. Of these, 12 credits are part of the Music Performance core taken by every Berklee student, which includes private instruction, ensembles, and labs that are designed to develop specific skills. A list of EDI-specific labs and ensembles is offered in Table 3.1.

One of the most important goals of the program is to provide a context for skills developed throughout the Berklee core music experience that focuses on harmony, ear training, and arranging skills. As students may enter the program with experience in performing and producing using a wide range of devices, including a DJ controller, Compact Disk Jockey (CDJ), or a turntable that does not easily produce discrete pitches, all students are expected to develop the skills to play a full range of pitched musical parts, such as melody, chordal accompaniment, bass, textural, and rhythm.

Table 3.1 A sample of the EDI curriculum requirements at Berklee College of Music

EDI experience	Semester 1	Semester 2	Semester 3	Semester 4
Private Instruction	1 or 2*	2	1	1
Instrumental Skills	1*	0	0	0
Labs	0	0	1	1
Ensembles	1	1	1	1
Total credits	**3**	**3**	**3**	**3**

Note: * Students take a half-hour lesson and keyboard fundamentals unless they pass a placement exam for keyboard proficiency, in which case they will have two credits of private instruction in their first semester.

The Curriculum

All students at Berklee take four semesters of study in a performance core that includes private instruction, instrumental labs, and ensembles. At this point, students in the EDI program take four semesters to complete their core music studies before going into their major. Most instrumentalists at Berklee have the option of choosing performance as their major and take eight semesters of lessons, labs, ensembles, and recital preparation classes. The courses lead to a Bachelor of Music in Performance, but for now, that option is not available to EDI players. Outside of Performance, and Music Education, which require six semesters of performance studies, EDI students can declare any other major at Berklee. As we gain experience in developing a pedagogical path to mastery of the EDI as part of performance practice, we will expand the program into an eight-semester performance major.[5]

Building Musicianship

We define levels of skill by specific musical capabilities and the level of development in a student's personal performance system. At the first level, a single keyboard controller is required. Conversely, at the fourth level, their system should include three controllers and an external hardware device such as a drum machine, synthesizer module, or step-sequencer. For all our students, we expect fluency in playing pitched music using both a keyboard controller and a grid controller such as an Ableton Push. In the first semester, all entering EDI students have a 30-minute private lesson and take a keyboard fundamentals class, unless they pass a keyboard proficiency exam, in which case they would take a 50-minute private lesson. While students in other principal instrument programs will take a 50-minute private lesson in their first semester, we view basic keyboard skills as part of instrumental development for EDI players, and the structure of this class

Table 3.2 The semester grid for the EDI Principal Instrument Program at Berklee College of Music

Course name	Credits	Course type
Performance Controller Studies	1	Lab
EDI Reading Lab 1	1	Lab
Live Looping Lab	1	Lab
Expressive Control Lab	1	Lab
Drum Machine Performance Lab	1	Lab
Rhythmic Foundations for Electronic Musicians	1	Lab
EDI Reading Lab 2	1	Lab
Vocal Processing Lab	1	Lab
Live Remix and Mashup Lab	1	Lab
Finger Drumming Techniques	1	Lab
Grid Controller Studies	1	Instrumental Studies
Modular Synthesizer Performance Studies	1	Instrumental Studies
Electronic Performance Seminar	1	Instrumental Studies
Women in Electronic Music	1	Instrumental Studies
DJ Techniques for EDI Players and Music Producers	1	Instrumental Studies
Electronic Improvisation	1	Ensemble
Downtempo Electronic Ensemble	1	Ensemble
Mashup Performance Ensemble	1	Ensemble
Future Pop Ensemble	1	Ensemble
Electronic Hip Hop and R&B Ensemble	1	Ensemble
Global Electronic Music Ensemble	1	Ensemble
Baroque Synthesizer Performance Ensemble	1	Ensemble
Electronic Performance Workshop Ensemble	1	Ensemble
EDI Showcase Ensemble	1	Ensemble
The Music of Disclosure	1	Ensemble

Note: Students take a half-hour lesson and keyboard fundamentals unless they pass a placement exam for keyboard proficiency, in which case they will have two credits of private instruction in their first semester.

would replace the time spent in a private lesson developing these skills (see Table 3.2).

The keyboard fundamentals class for EDI principals is patterned after the Berklee Online course, *Keyboard for the Electronic Musician*. The course is designed to develop practical skills for playing musical parts with a keyboard controller rather than building traditional two-handed piano technique. It is ideally suited for the needs of an EDI player. Students who have had piano lessons at some point in their musical development often hold sufficient keyboard literacy skills to place out of the keyboard fundamentals class. For many students who take the class, it is also an opportunity to begin to develop reading skills and to make connections between the Berklee core music program and instrumental performance. Over the course of the semester, students in the class learn keyboard fingerings, including scales, chord construction, and reading. Because most entering EDI players have used a keyboard controller for MIDI sequencing, many will not have the dexterity to use it in a musical performance and will need this time to develop this skill.

Levels of Proficiency

The EDI program is based on four levels of proficiency. At each level, students will develop skills to perform scales, chords, and rhythm parts in addition to a prepared piece. They are required to demonstrate music technology skills for each level, such as session management, controller mapping, and troubleshooting. Early in the program, we stress the need to develop a standard template that gives students a collection of sound resources they can use as a point of departure in practice, lab, and ensemble settings. While as a producer they may be able to take their time finding the perfect sound for a production, the culture of performance really requires them to be ready to take on a variety of roles immediately, so software synthesizers need to be instantiated in this personal template, ready to play melody, bass, and percussion parts as well as loops, samples, and a variety of other sounds. Here, students are encouraged to develop their own voice while being able to fulfill a range of musical functions on call.

Certainly, one of the goals of the EDI Program is for students to develop a level of mastery on their instrument. Since the player designs their own instrument to a large extent, we define mastery as the ability to control a fully developed system that is made up of multiple controllers performing a variety of musical roles. Everyone will enter the program with a degree of proficiency in using at least one controller, most often a keyboard or grid controller. From there, we expect them to develop a system of at least three controllers and an additional hardware device, and levels of proficiency are defined accordingly.

We expect students to be able to play major and minor scales, individual chords, and common chord progressions in all keys using both a keyboard controller and a grid controller. In the first level of proficiency, all students focus on developing these skills using a keyboard controller, and they use a grid controller for the second level. From the third level on, students are expected to choose one of these to further develop their skill in playing melodic and harmonic parts. All rhythmic proficiencies are expected to be demonstrated using a grid controller. Student progress is assessed at the end of each semester in a proficiency exam that is administered by a team of two faculty members who are not the student's private lesson instructors. A final private lesson grade for the semester is made up of the final exam grade and the private lesson instructor's own assessment.

While basic keyboard fingerings are well developed, we are only just learning how to develop skills using a grid controller with pedagogy that follows the common practice of established players. At one level, the goal is to develop pure physical dexterity, but we expect students to navigate a variety of musical and technical functions with a grid controller. A player will need to play melodic and harmonic passages, percussion patterns, control transport, and various software functions. Although most mass-marketed grid controllers map pads to specific software functions in a DAW, a grid can ultimately be configured in any number of ways. A player can customize their controller for unique capabilities specific to the individual's performance practice, and exploring these options needs to be part of the EDI pedagogy.

Digital Grid Controller Pedagogy

Grid controllers can be used to fulfill melodic and harmonic functions, and there are several different ways to do this. A grid can usually be set to a chromatic mode, where each pad represents a half-step movement, much like keys on a piano. Pads light up to indicate instances of the tonic note, serving as a reference. In a chromatic mode, pads can also display notes on a scale, leaving notes not in a scale unlit. Pads can also be set to a scale mode, where all pads will trigger notes in a particular scale. Any pad played will trigger a note in a defined scale, much like a diatonic harmonica. Either of these arrangements allows a player to develop virtuosity quickly, as the mapping of notes to pads is the same for any diatonic scale. At Berklee, we focus on learning scales in chords in a chromatic mode so that any chromatic, non-scale note is available to the player in a key. Mappings for all keys and many types of scales are available as presets in most grid controllers, and the ability to access and change these in a performance is a skill the player needs to develop (see Figure 3.1).

There are two philosophies guiding the development of physical dexterity in playing a grid controller. Using two hands allows learners to develop speed and agility in playing melodic and rhythmic parts. If the player's goal is to develop a level of virtuosity, this is the approach they will take. However, with a multi-controller configuration, a player may need to have a high degree of right/left-hand independence, where one hand is playing a musical passage while the other is adjusting synthesizer parameters, mixing settings, or enabling DAW controls such as loop recording. This type of left/right-hand independence is an important part of a musician's development

Figure 3.1 An example of a faculty member from Berklee College of Music
performing with electronic digital instruments. Used with permission by
the performer and artist Dávid Bodnár.

and requires quite a bit of practice. While physical hand independence is
required to play a single musical idea on many instruments, an EDI player
needs to develop a kind of cognitive independence to carry out these types
of simultaneous functions.

The Berklee Performance Core for EDI Players

As with any other instrument at Berklee, proficiency is developed through
a student's experience in a combination of labs, ensembles, and private lessons. Ideally, these will work together to foster a student's musical development. Ensemble experiences allow students to develop repertoire in
small groups with other instrumentalists. While an EDI-only ensemble is
one option for these players, a key part of a student's development comes
from playing with other instrumentalists, especially since many EDI players
come from a production background and have not had this type of musical
experience. Students develop specific skills in labs that cover techniques
such as live looping, mash-up, remix, and finger drumming. In private lessons, students work on specific skills needed at each of the four levels of

proficiency, including repertoire selection, individual instrument design, and developing their musical identity.

Future Directions

We recognize that we are only beginning to develop a pedagogy for the EDI program at Berklee. Many challenges and opportunities remain ahead of us. For example, sight reading is an important skill for any musician, but how we develop this in an EDI player is still an open question. We currently expect students to develop a basic level of reading ability through keyboard skills and core music classes, but focused practice in this area is currently not a focus of the program. The question of notation looms large, and while standard notation works well with keyboard performance, it may not be as useful in developing exercises for grid controllers. Some of the same issues we face in developing a system of notation for synthesizers also remain for the EDI, and with controlling a myriad of software functions such an important part of electronic performance, adding numerous types of instructions in a clear way can be a challenge.

Perhaps the most challenging part of our work moving forward is that it will be a never-ending process. As technology develops, the EDI will also change. Glove controllers, brainwave sensors, and machine learning are important parts of ongoing development that will soon make their way to the mass market. They will rapidly transform the practice of electronic music performance. Given this, an overarching goal of our program is to develop players who can adapt and evolve with technology, keeping the core of musical knowledge as they develop at the center of their practice, and the curiosity to embrace new ways of approaching performance in the future.

As we expand our notion of instrumental performance and musical training in higher education, significant questions remain about how to best serve all students going forward. Technical knowledge of analog and digital audio fundamentals, sound synthesis, sound design, and electronic production techniques are at the core of what an EDI instrumentalist needs to know and demonstrate. At what point does the depth of knowledge and experience in these areas become required of all music students to prepare them to be successful? Are we creating two distinct classes of musicians based on technical skill and instrument proficiency? If we acknowledge that the computer plays a central role in developing a comprehensive view of contemporary musical practice, then all musicians should have the skills to use technology as a platform for learning music and pursuing a career in the music industry. If we look at how the piano has traditionally been the point of reference for developing an understanding of music, we see that one does not need to be a virtuoso pianist to excel in any area of music. Likewise, while we will see virtuoso EDI performers and producers, all musicians should embrace the skills that make those means of expression unique to contemporary music.

And finally, what components of traditional music education will become specialized areas of study as emerging skill sets become essential? At Berklee, we have approached this question in our curriculum by providing students with a study of harmony that develops an understanding of contemporary song forms and jazz composition, along with studies in traditional harmony and counterpoint. While one can argue that pursuing both is good for any student, we see that traditional harmony and counterpoint support studies in composition for concert music and film scoring, while the Berklee harmony curriculum provides the foundation for songwriting. However, as technology fuels the development of new forms such as hip hop and electronic dance music, we need to move beyond an understanding of music rooted in the piano keyboard. Here, the development of the EDI as a complete instrument may provide some insight into where music education is heading. In whatever way we answer these questions, musicians have always paved the way for innovation in musical practice, and contemporary musicians should guide us in our thinking going forward on what is essential in music education.

Reflection Questions

1. How can we use the EDI to inspire musical literacy in underserved communities?
2. Since an EDI is often made up of multiple devices and continually evolves as a player develops, what does it mean to practice in this medium? Are there exercises that are common for all players? Is it useful to model practice routines using existing sources for other instruments? How and in what ways?
3. At what point do we consider a Bachelor of Music Degree program that does not require that a student play any kind of instrument and recognizes a well-educated producer as a fully formed musician?
4. Academic accreditation for a school to grant a Bachelor of Music Degree is based on a traditional model of music education. How could this be adapted to support an EDI-centric music program?

Notes

1 Although DAWs are designed to record real-time keyboard performances as MIDI events, many electronic producers add individual notes by drawing them into the timeline or piano roll. Producer Deadmau5 uses this method since he is

not a keyboard player. Other artists such as Venetian Squares and Aphex Twin draw MIDI events to create complex rhythmic patterns that would be difficult or nearly impossible to play.

2 Berklee was founded in 1945 as Schillinger House by Lawrence Berk to provide working musicians the opportunity to advance their musical skills with practical training in playing and writing popular music rooted in the jazz tradition.

3 The Berklee Cirque du Soleil Ensemble is one example of how EDI players can play an important role in contemporary performance practice. Music directors for all Cirque du Soleil shows use Ableton Live to conduct a live ensemble, providing tempo, cues, additional musical parts, and sound effects. The Berklee ensemble uses Ableton Live sessions from selected shows, giving students the opportunity to model this real-world performance experience (https://youtu.be/DsHGFOzySIY).

4 Although the Berklee audition is the same for all instruments, we felt the need to clarify our expectations specifically for EDI players, who in many cases have not been prepared to audition for a college music program. We make it clear that students need to demonstrate live performance skills, and not their productions (https://college.berklee.edu/admissions/undergraduate/electronic-digital-instrument-guidelines).

5 There are variety of degree pathways for the EDI instrumentalist at Berklee. Most of them are publicly available at: www.berklee.edu/sites/default/files/d7/bcm/07%20BM4_ELPD_2020.pdf.

References

Berklee College of Music. (n.d.). *Mission and philosophy*. Retrieved June 10, 2021, from https://www.berklee.edu/about/mission-and-philosophy.

Berklee Online. (n.d.). *Keyboard for the electronic musician*. Retrieved June 10, 2021, from https://online.berklee.edu/courses/keyboard-for-the-electronic-musician.

Keith, S. (2010, June). Bridging the gap: Thoughts on computer music and contemporary (popular) electronic music. In *Proceedings of the 2010 Australasian computer music conference* (pp. 37–42). The Basin, Australia: The Australasian Computer Music Association.

Tobias, E. S. (2013). Composing, songwriting, and producing: Informing popular music pedagogy. *Research Studies in Music Education*, *35*(2), 213–237. https://doi.org/10.1177/0027432113483318.

4   Behind the Music

Digital Music Instrument Ensembles

David A. Williams

Introduction

On January 27, 2010, Steve Jobs first introduced the iPad at an Apple press conference at the Yerba Buena Center for the Arts in San Francisco. In a new category of devices referred to as table computers, the iPad was released on April 3 of the same year. This led to two events that inspired me to become a digital musician and create music in a digital music ensemble.

The first was an Apple commercial that aired on TV. The 30-second commercial included footage of a guitar app being played (see Figure 4.1). The guitar video was only on the iPad screen for about three seconds, but it was long enough to get my attention. I realized that this new iPad device enabled musicians to perform music in new and innovative ways.

The second event was an internal grant program announced by my employer, the University of South Florida. The grant was called the "Innovative Teaching Opportunities with iPads Grant" and was a competitive program aimed at helping faculty integrate iPads into their teaching and research. In May 2010, I was awarded the grant, which allowed for the purchase of five iPads, five Altec Lansing Orbit MP3 speakers, and some musical apps. This grant funding also provided the equipment needed to start an iPad band in the Fall of 2011. The initial group members, all music faculty, named the group Touch. While the makeup of the band has changed over the past decade, we have taken on a variety of different projects and we continue to make music. We are digital musicians. We are iPadists.

Context and Background

To understand the significance of all this for me, we have to look back at my musical background. In the seventh grade I was a clarinet player. I also played tenor saxophone. I grew up performing in school bands. Concert bands, marching bands, and jazz bands – bands – but no popular music

DOI: 10.4324/9781003216728-5

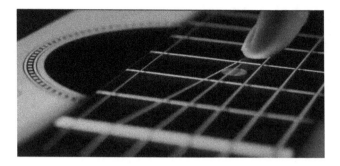

Figure 4.1 The guitar in Apple's GarageBand application for the iPad (from a commercial created by Apple, Inc. for the reveal of the second-generation iPad).

groups. No rock bands, or punk bands. No rhythm and blues, or heavy metal, or funk, or reggae, or pop. When I performed on the clarinet or saxophone, I was really never asked to play something by ear, nor was I asked to compose original music. There was always printed music, composed by someone else, to read from. There was always a conductor or director, who stood in front of the group, and they made the musical and creative decisions for the students. Rarely (if ever) was I involved in selecting the music we performed. I was a pawn in the music education tradition that has existed for nearly a hundred years.

After high school, I earned a Bachelor's degree in music education and became a music teacher/conductor. I rarely performed on the clarinet or saxophone any longer. Instead, I conducted school bands. Concert bands, marching bands, and jazz bands – bands – but no popular music groups. No rock bands, or punk bands. No rhythm and blues, or heavy metal, or funk, or reggae, or pop. I really never asked students to play something by ear, nor did I ask them to compose original music. I always handed out printed music that was composed by someone else. I made the musical and creative decisions for students, and I selected the music we performed. I perpetuated the music education tradition.

None of this bothered me. Yet.

It was with this background as a performing musician, and as a music teacher, that I started a band. Not a concert band, but a popular music band. A band that would end up performing music from a wide variety of musical styles, including rock, punk, rhythm and blues, heavy metal, funk, reggae, and pop. A band that would not read notation on sheet music but created and performed originally composed music. A band that would require collaborative creativity from all its members. It is important to understand how unprepared I was for this. In fact, because of my musical background, I could not have been less prepared. Even with over three decades of involvement in formal music education, I was not prepared for this experience. And I had no idea what I was in for.

What follows is the story of the band Touch.

Digital Musicianship

Since its inception and for more than a decade, Touch has existed as five musicians playing iPads as musical instruments. In more refined musical involvements, we would have been considered a chamber group performing chamber music. But we have been a band. We "practiced" instead of "rehearsed." We performed "shows" instead of "concerts." And we regularly included vocalists, dancers, actors, visual artists, poets, video and lighting effects, and haze in our shows. We also involved the audience as collaborators and participants on a regular basis. We covered popular music songs and created original music. And we have never printed a concert program!

Touch began with five School of Music faculty members: two from music education, two composers, and a music theorist. My four band mates all had some type of previous musical involvement as part of a popular music group. All except me, of course. At the time, none of us knew what iPads were, but we were interested in finding out what we could do with them. We first started meeting together as a group once per week for about an hour. These early meetings were exploratory in design, as they often consisted of "show and tell" moments, where we shared new music apps we had found with each other. Everyone would download an app, and we would often spend the rest of our time together playing with it. We played with the sounds. We were not rehearsing anything. We were practicing being musical, but in a different way than most traditional conceptions. At the time, I really did not think much about it. But in retrospect, we were learning a lot about music. Above all else, we were having fun playing around with new toys (apps), sounds, timbres, techniques, and, importantly, emerging musical possibilities. We were totally engrossed in the sounds we were creating. We were being creative. Every now and then, four of us would hear a band mate make a new sound, and we were all over them: "What was that?" "How did you do that?" "What is that app called?" Importantly, we collaborated. At some points, someone would play something and others would join in with different parts, different sounds, different pitches.

We were making music as a group in ways that were antithetical to anything I had previously experienced as a musician and educator. In retrospect, it is interesting that in these moments I did not think much about what we were doing. In my previous musical life, my concert band life, I would have considered this wasted time. But it was not wasted. In fact, it might have been some of the most musically involved time I have spent with others in a group. We were playing with sound (and silence) in a very personal way, and at the core, isn't that what music making should be about? We went through periods of intense concentration, discussion, and times when we laughed hard together. But we were never wasting a second. There was musical growth going on like I had never experienced before. Growth in the understanding of music as sound. Not notes on a page to be re-created.

And there it is. With this musical growth, my past began to haunt me. I was not prepared for learning like this. I felt like an elementary-age child encountering my first creative musical experiences within formal music education. Except I did not have as much wonder and amazement as a second-grader might. Instead, I was mostly filled with dread. None of this was true for my colleagues. They had done this before during their (outside of school) popular music performance experiences. There were times when I simply could not keep up with the group. They would start jamming away in an improvisatory experiment, and I would sit there wondering. What chords are these? What's the harmonic rhythm? What should I play? I just couldn't hear it. More than three decades of formal music education behind me, and I could not hear and emulate a simple chord progression. I needed printed music to read from, but there wasn't any. If music is made up of sound and silence, there were times I did only the silence. Too many times.

Let me remind you. Since the seventh grade I was a clarinet and saxophone player. I grew up in school bands. Concert bands, marching bands, and jazz bands – bands – but no popular music groups. No rock bands, or punk bands. No rhythm and blues, or heavy metal, or funk, or reggae, or pop. As part of the bands in which I performed clarinet, I was really never asked to play something by ear, nor was I asked to create original music. There was always printed music, composed by someone else, to read from. And there was always a conductor or director who made the musical and creative decisions for the students. Rarely (if ever) did I select music I would perform.

And none of this bothered me. Then. But now it was a real bother.

Regardless, I plugged along. I was determined to get better at this type of music making. After all, I was in a band. A band that was different than any band I had previously experienced. Importantly, I was having fun and enjoying my experiences. Bothered, but still having fun. I looked forward to our times together making music. Even though I am sure I was a bother to my bandmates sometimes, they were kind to me (most of the time) and put up with my musical inadequacies. On reflection, it reminds me of the neighborhood kid who was lousy at baseball, but the other kids let him play anyway – since he was the one who owned the bat and the ball. I was the one who obtained the iPads!

The First Performance and New Possibilities

As the weeks went by, we did not share new apps quite as often but began playing music regularly. We covered songs we liked and created some original material. Sometimes a band member would bring an idea for a piece with them, and we would start collaboratively creating something on the spot. It did not take long before we had somewhat of a set-list. We had a few covers, so we needed to add vocalists. We had some soundscape pieces, so we needed to add dancers and actors. We also had some electronic music pieces that stood on their own.

Then it happened. A turning point for Touch. At one of our practice sessions, a band member said, "We should schedule a performance date in our concert hall and put on a show." I had never previously considered something like a performance. We were scheduled to conduct a workshop at an upcoming Florida Music Education Association Professional Development Conference, and as part of this session we would perform some music. However, the idea of presenting a full-length show had not been considered as a group until that moment. However, everyone agreed, and we made plans to organize a concert. We recruited two music major vocalists, and we reached out to the School of Theatre & Dance to begin collaborating with dancers and actors.

Our first show was held in March 2012 and was a success.[1] The venue was nearly full, and the band kept the audience entertained the entire evening. Of all things, we kicked it off with a cover of "Smoke on the Water." We also performed several originals, including some with audience interaction and a 15-minute improvisatory piece with dance (see Figure 4.2). In preparation for the performance of the dance piece, we spent hours with ten dancers imagining sounds and movements. The final "score" included five three-minute sections that alternated between having an obvious beat and no beat. Along with video, lighting effects, and haze, the piece was a full-on sensory experience that was a true collaboration in every sense of the word. This show also included a rendition of the children's book, *Where the Wild Things Are*, as a narrator read the text, and we created music to evoke moods and themes from the text. In addition, we had three actors who visually realized the text in real time.

These two collaborative pieces were the first of many for the band. Looking back over all the band has done during the past decade, I have to say it is the collaborations with other artists that have been the most rewarding. They were also the most demanding in terms of time and effort but

Figure 4.2 A live performance by Touch at the University of South Florida. Image
courtesy of the author.

without a doubt, the greatest opportunities for originality. There is something special in collaborating to make art with other types of artists. Many
of the discussions and practices we have had were nothing short of magi-
cal. Musicians can learn a lot from dancers, actors, and visual artists, and
I would like to think it goes the other way around as well. The music education profession could greatly enhance the artistic growth of students by
regularly involving them in collaborative work with other artists.

Learner-Centered Pedagogical Approach

After our first year, a music education colleague in the group and I decided
to include only individuals associated with music education. For this reason,
we changed personnel by replacing our non-music education band members
with three music education graduate students. We did this primarily because
we wanted the band to be an example of our music education program
regarding the collaborative model we were using in the group. Although
I was not aware of it at the time, I know now that we were modeling what
could be called a learner-centered pedagogical approach to learning music.
Over the past decade, we have continued to embody this approach in a fair
amount of our undergraduate and graduate music education courses. Touch
continues to provide a visible (and aural!) model outside the curriculum.

It is important to understand that this model has nothing to do with the
instruments used by Touch (iPads). A learner-centered approach to music
learning is not about the instruments. It also is not about digital technology.
We could be using violins and oboes and still practice a learner-centered
approach to learning. Such an approach typically involves students working
collaboratively in several small groups (instead of one large group). The

focus of learning tends to be creativity (instead of performance). Students have significant autonomy over music choice and instruments, and they are the ones making most, if not all, of the musical and creative decisions (instead of the teacher or leader). In addition, music tends to be learned through an aural process (instead of through notation). The other important difference between a learner-centered approach and the typical teacher-centered model historically used in music education has to do with the role of the teacher: to provide open-ended assignments and help students when they need it (instead of directing the entire learning process).

In short, a learner-centered approach turns over much of the work of learning to the students and places them in charge of their own learning.[2] Students are asked to do a good deal of what traditionally has been done by the teacher or leader. As Doyle (2008) states:

> Why should teachers change to a learner-centered approach to instruction? The answer is actually very simple. Fifteen years of neuroscience, biology, and cognitive psychology research findings on how humans learn offer this powerful and singular conclusion: It is the one who does the work who does the learning.

Collaborations and Outcomes

Beginning in our second year, Touch continued to maintain a learner-centered approach and serve as an active model for music education students regarding an alternative to music making outside traditional large ensembles. There were several highlights for the band during this period. One of my favorites remains a collaboration we did with actors from the School of Theatre & Dance. In collaboration with audience members, we re-told the story of *The Wizard of Oz*. The audience was asked to tweet what they would like to see happen next in our story. Their tweets, through a live Twitter feed, were displayed on a large projection screen on stage. The actors combined various audience suggestions and improvised these on stage, all while the band played background music and sound effects to fit the mood, as well as original arrangements of *Oz* songs at critical moments.

Another example of audience participation involved an original piece during which audience members, who brought their own devices (tablet or phone), performed with the band. The audience was asked to bring a device preloaded with a specific app (Bebot). Interestingly, many did. As we performed the piece, audience members were split into three different groups and each one was "conducted" by a dancer from the stage. At another show, the audience became involved with a visual artist during a collaboration between the artist and the band. During this piece, the artist was on one side of the stage and painted the band members in performance. Individual band members, on the other side of the stage, took their cues for when they could play based on which colors of paint the artist was using at any given point. The audience began shouting words of encouragement to the artist and then counted down with the timer as the seven minutes was coming to an end. The painting still hangs in my office. This particular piece, by the way, was the winning composition resulting from a contest we sponsored for an original piece for iPads.

In every show Touch has given, the audience has played an active role throughout by clapping along with a beat, dancing, and interacting with band members between songs. We talk to the audience between songs, and they soon begin to feel free to interact. One of the goals for the band is to remove the artificial "fourth wall" that is most often placed between the stage and the audience in traditional music education concerts. We would rather the audience feel like they are a part of the show. In our most recent shows, we include a question-and-answer session near the end of the evening so that audience members can ask us questions about what we are doing on stage. We have found that the audience really enjoys the opportunity to interact.

Some other interesting pieces we have done include an original piece that revolved around poetry, written and read by four poets from our Department of English. One at a time the poets gave live readings and were assigned an iPadist, along with one or more dancers, who realized their poems in sound and movement. The piece continued after the live readings by means of a pre-recorded video that combined segments of each poem into a visual montage. The band continued to play original music as the video was presented, and the individual dancers all combined in a visual display. Another show featured students from a local high school dance program in a "history of dance" piece that included examples of gavotte, waltz, jitterbug, tap, rumba, samba, disco, improvisation, and hip hop. And finally, another collaboration featured actors from our School of Theatre & Dance who improvised their way through a modern version of *Beauty and the Beast*. The band created original music for the piece and added sound effects to enhance the mood set by the actors. The piece ended up engaging the audience several times as the actors continually moved off the stage and into the house.

Every Touch show has had a theme, or at minimum, a title. We presented *Like Nothing You've Seen* and the *Louder Than Ever Before* shows. We have also presented shows partnered with area and national organizations which, in part, served as fundraising efforts and/or attempts to raise awareness. For example, our *BePartOfTheSolution* show was in coordination with Hope For Justice and the International Justice Mission, two organizations dedicated to bringing an end to modern slavery – an issue that is far too prevalent in our area. *The Love Concert* benefitted area homeless veterans and was held in conjunction with the National Initiative for Arts & Health in the Military 2017 National Summit. Touch has also done two Contemporary Christian shows, including a Christmas Worship Concert.

In addition to numerous appearances in our local community and on our home university campus, Touch has been invited and/or selected to perform at several state and national conferences. We have played at state music education associations in Florida, Texas, and Missouri, at the 2014 National Association for Music Education National In-Service Conference in Nashville, the 2015 Florida Educational Technology Conference in Orlando, the 2016 College Music Society National Conference in Santa Fe, New Mexico, the 2018 National Association for Schools of Music Annual Meeting in Washington, DC, the 2019 National Association for Music Education National Conference in Orlando, Florida, and the 2020 College Music Society National Conference (online). The band has also played at two TEDx events and was featured on an ESPN segment.

Conclusion

Through all of this, the practice of Touch has remained the same.[3] Band members still use iPads as musical instruments. Most weeks, we play together for 60–75 minutes, with additional time working on collaborations as needed. Our time together tends to be relaxed, fun, and set in a learner-centered model where the sounds (instruments/apps) used are the decision of each individual. Also, everyone has the opportunity to provide creative input at any time, and our musical work continues to happen through aural means.

For the past three years, Touch has been made up of undergraduate music education students and myself. Now I get to delight in watching students grow musically in ways similar to what I have experienced. The students see their own musical growth as well, and they certainly recognize the value of the learner-centered approach used with Touch. Two recent experiences were particularly noteworthy. One student, a horn player in traditional ensembles, was playing bass for the band. During a sound check before a recent show, she was playing by herself and the sound resonating in the room was extremely powerful (by the way, our concerts are loud!). She stopped, looked at me, and, with great animation, said, "I feel like a god!" She further explained that she had never felt as significant in prior music-related activities. Another student, who had played drums for Touch, reflected on his sense of significance in the band. Having just graduated, he reported that he "had never felt as vital to a musical group before," and "for the first time I felt I had a really important role in an ensemble."

Personally, I have continued to struggle as an aural musician, but I am getting better. I find I am continually able to hear things that I didn't hear before. I am better at hearing chord progressions. I've found this progression as an aural musician to be more exciting than any of my previous musical experiences. I considered myself an excellent musician before. As a high school clarinet player, I was selected for four all-state bands. As a band director, I produced outstanding-sounding bands. But the musical satisfaction is now much deeper than I felt before.

With each passing experience, I am left to wonder what my musical life might have been like if my middle school and high school music teachers had provided learner-centered experiences for me. If they would have furnished opportunities in which I had autonomy over instrument and music choice, where I was the one making creative decisions working collaboratively with other musicians and artists, and where I was forced to use my ears more than my eyes. I can only imagine that my personal musicianship would have grown more than it did, and my sense of significance and importance, as a musician, would be greater. I am also left to wonder how many current students in middle school and high school have music teachers that could be providing such experiences and opportunities for them today.

Reflection Questions

1. What are some opportunities for including learner-centered pedagogical techniques in secondary music education classes?
2. How might music teachers allow students to become creative musicians?
3. In what musical settings can music teachers add to their students' sense of significance and importance?
4. What needs to happen for the music education profession to fully embrace digital musical instruments and musicians in school music programs?
5. How can music teachers (and students) become more involved in artistic collaboration with other artists, including dancers, actors, visual artists, poets, and architects?

Notes

1 Here are two video examples of Touch shows: "iPad Concert (Touch)" (www .youtube.com/watch?v=Mf87gB7fieI) and "The iPad as a musical instrument: Touch (the USF faculty iPad band) at TEDxTampaBay" (www.youtube.com/ watch?v=wYoEAjt27yc).

2 For a more complete understanding of learner-centered pedagogy, check out the following: Burvall, A., & Ryder, D. (2017). *Intention: Critical creativity in the classroom*. Irvine, CA: EdTech Team Press. Sulla, N. (2019). *Students taking charge in grades 6–12: Inside the learner-active, technology-infused classroom*. New York: Routledge. Williams, D., & Kladder, J. R. (2020). *The leaner-centered music classroom: Models and possibilities*. New York: Routledge.

3 To see information concerning equipment and apps used by Touch, see: Williams, D. (2021). The iPad as a musical instrument. In Greher, G. R., & Burton, S. L. (Eds.), *Creative music making at your fingertips: A mobile technology guide for music educators*. New York: Oxford University Press.

Reference

Doyle, T. (2008). *Helping students learn in a learner-centered environment: A guide to facilitating learning in higher education*. Sterling, VA: Stylus.

5   The Popular Music Vocal Studio

Considerations for Creating an Effective Curriculum

Kat Reinhert

Introduction

As higher popular music education (HPME) programs continue to make their way into academia, it is important to consider the different skills and knowledge vocalists moving through these programs will require upon graduation (Bartlett & Naismith, 2020; Bennett, 2007; Hughes et al., 2013a, 2013b; Hughes, 2017; Moir et al., 2019, Smith et al., 2017, Reinhert, 2018, 2019). Vocalists in HPME programs may have a variety of distinctive career and artistic goals. Some may want to use their voices in recording careers or as background vocalists for established artists, while others may want to work as songwriters and/or performers of their own original music. Yet other students may work in the service industry, such as club dates, weddings, or on cruise ships. Others might choose a career as a voice-over artist in the film and television industry. Often, these performance careers will overlap with one another and with non-performing music industry jobs, shaping what is known as a portfolio career: a non-conventional career path whose foundation is not based on a single position or area of expertise. Rather, it is a career path constructed on a diversity of areas of knowledge and proficiencies, both in and out of the performative realm (Bennett, 2012, 2013; Reinhert, 2017; Scott & Scott, 2017; Smith, 2013; Williams & Williams, 2017).

Popular music singing is a subset of contemporary commercial music styles of singing (American Association for Teachers of Singing; 2009; Benson, 2020; Hoch, 2018; Leborgne & Rosenberg, 2014; Reinhert, 2017, 2019). For the purpose of this chapter, a popular music vocalist (PMV) is defined as one who sings music not categorized as classical, jazz, or musical theatre. Although jazz and musical theatre overlap with popular music in many areas of vocal music, including vocal technique, history, and knowledge, this chapter is concerned with specific considerations surrounding the popular music voice studio (PMVS). Furthermore, this chapter assumes

DOI: 10.4324/9781003216728-6

that the PMVS would be housed within an HPME degree program and not as an independent voice program or as a studio within a larger traditional voice program. This is because popular music vocalists require a skillset and knowledgebase found outside a traditional voice program (Bartlett & Naismith, 2020; Hoch, 2018, Leborgne & Rosenberg, 2014; Reinhert, 2019). As many of these experiences would not fit into the curriculum within a PMVS setting alone, it is assumed that the HPME coursework and the PMVS would provide the necessary skills and knowledge in tandem with each other. This chapter will explore these considerations, examine how working with students within these spaces is necessarily different but can provide myriad new ways toward artistic expression, consider culture, explore assessment possibilities, and provide possible aspects to include in the creation of a curriculum for PMVS within a larger HPME program.

Creating the Curriculum: An Adaptive Curricular Framework

Considering how to create an adaptable curricular framework with room for individual expression and exploration is important within educational spaces (Bartlett & Naismith, 2020; Hess, 2019; Hughes, 2017; Khan & Law,

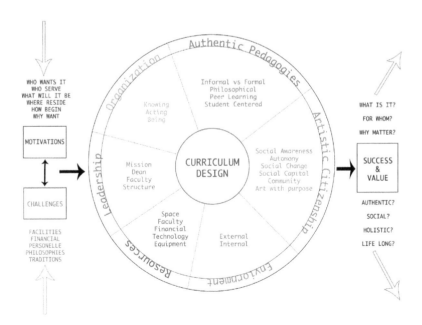

Figure 5.1 Conceptual framework for HPME curriculum (from Reinhert, 2018).

2015; Lebler & Weston, 2015; Reinhert, 2018, 2019). An adaptable curricular framework includes some basic considerations that will help structure the overall breadth and depth of the curriculum itself (see Figure 5.1). On the left of Figure 5.1, different motivations and challenges shape how the curriculum is designed. Once these concepts are discussed and arrived upon, the curriculum becomes the focus of construction. The inner wheel represents the interconnected aspects, where all parts lead to the center and the center leads to all parts, indicating a continual and evolving relationship between the parts and the whole. Moving out of the wheel, yet also affecting its design, are philosophies about success and value. Ideally, each of the parts of this wheel would affect some aspect of curricular construction (Reinhert, 2018).

Developing an adaptive curriculum necessitates encouraging individuality while simultaneously helping to develop each student's voice. In this way, curricula would ideally align with the larger HPME program. The music and concepts taught in the HPME program would also be taught in the studio and vice versa. Therefore, the studio would not be a siloed learning environment but provide students with a holistic learning experience, mirroring real-world interactions and experiences whenever possible. Tables 5.1 and 5.2 move through the conceptual framework with practical applications for considerations in this regard.

Table 5.1 offers a goal – an intended ending point – with all the parts of the curriculum examined. Table 5.2 offers an example of how these ideas could manifest further in the curriculum.

Considering Pedagogy: How Popular Musicians Learn

Creativity is often a messy process, and creative people often learn things by "figuring things out" on their own (Kaufman & Gregoire, 2016). This kind of "messy" learning, sometimes referred to in educational spaces as informal learning, was investigated by Green (2002). Green (2002) found that informal learning is very common for popular musicians and is often embedded within the creative process. Often, in these home-based learning environments, music learning is self-directed and self-motivated: the musician chooses the musical selections without the help of a teacher (Lebler, 2007).

Students within HPME programs tend to be these kinds of self-motivated learners with a keen sense of what they want to get out of their education, often with a variety of skills, abilities, and musical backgrounds. Some will have had many years of formal music training before attending college, while others may have a wide range of traditional musical experiences from school learning (band/choir/orchestra) contexts. It is also possible that some will have had little or no formal music training. Instead, they

Table 5.1 Curricular components for a PMV curriculum

Topic	Description of attributes or experiences related to the topic area
Lessons	• Focused on repertoire replication • Learning the music that is being learned in the ensemble • Vocal health for a long career
Ensemble	• Focused on repertoire replication • Learning and performing music that is commonly performed in club date band settings
Theory/ear training	• Focused on chart writing • Focused on chord and harmony understanding • Lots of practical ear training (listening to a song and playing it completely by ear)
Musicology	• Focused on understanding the music that is being performed • Historical significance • Cultural significance
Entrepreneurship/music business	• Understanding contracts • Gig etiquette • Taxes • Appearance and marketing
Music tech	• Focus on understanding microphones and live sound
What's missing in this curriculum?	• Creative music making and original music creation • Improvisation • Student autonomy • Holistic understanding of music • Pedagogical awareness knowledge • No focus on playing any other instrument than main one • No DAW experiences • No engineering experience

will have learned to play and perform music from online sources, friends, or whatever they could figure out on their own (Green, 2006; Holley, 2019; Powell, 2011; Reinhert, 2018). Awareness of these diverse backgrounds and experiences is important for the creation of a successful PMVS curriculum, as it provides a background and awareness for creating a student-centered learning experience.

Shifting Power Dynamics: From Teacher to Facilitator

Within HPME programs, the PMVS teacher would ideally be a facilitator of knowledge and musical growth – someone who guides and mentors a

Table 5.2 Considerations guiding questions in developing a PMV curriculum

Motivation	• Prepare students for gigs in professional club date bands
Challenges	• Are there enough facilities and musicians to facilitate learning popular music in an authentic manner?
	• Do faculty have real-world experience in this space?
	• Does the commercial and popular music program align with the traditions of the school?
	• Are there enough financial resources to support all that is needed to adequately prepare students?
Framework	• A **hybrid combination**: employability + cultural
	• **Employability**: repertoire, harmonies, what to wear, tech, vocal load, placing the student in ensembles that prepare the repertoire appropriately
	• **Cultural**: helping students understand all the ins and outs of what this kind of life and gig entails – e.g., dealing with the clients, managing the set lists, the banter, making sure they get enough sleep and are taking care of their instrument, understanding the cultural significance of the music they are preparing to perform
Pedagogies	• **Formal**: Providing students with a repertoire list and telling them exactly how to perform each song
	• **Informal/peer/student-centered**: Providing students with a repertoire list and requiring them to learn material on their own – through recordings, with their ensemble, however they want to figure it out – with the teacher facilitating and helping when needed
Interactions	• Have students discussed how this type of gig engages with their community?
	• How can they be a leader in a service industry gig?
	• Discuss the space for artistic purpose within a club date band
	• Discuss whether they would accept a gig for a cause they didn't adhere to
Environment	• Is there a place where the student will be able to implement their skills once they achieve a professional level?
	• Is there an acceptance of this kind of gig within the university, as both valid and musical, at a professional level?
Resources	• Does the school have a room equipped with microphones, amps, monitors, etc. that is conducive to learning this repertoire authentically?
	• Does the school have faculty familiar with how these kinds of gigs actually work (lived experience) who can help students navigate this space?
	• Does the school have enough students to form this kind of ensemble and to learn music quickly and at a high level?
Leadership	• Does the course align with the mission of the school/program?
	• Does the dean support this program and its goals?
	• Do the faculty have the learned and experienced knowledge to understand the requirements for this kind of gig?
	• Is there a structure set up to help students succeed?

Success	• How is success measured? Is it just by the songs the students know, or is it an awareness and understanding of all the things that go into this kind of gig? And if a student does not want to learn a particular song, does that mean they will not have success?
Value	• What if a student has no interest in singing in a club date band, but they are in the program?
	• Does this curriculum provide the student with other skills, such as the ability to learn music on their own, create original music, work within a DAW, teach popular music to others, develop an understanding of how to help others learn popular music, develop an understanding of the empathy and kindness required to do service gigs regularly, how it affects the long-term usage of the voice, etc.?
	• Is there a social component embedded in the curriculum that helps students understand and connect to their local music community and the larger global music community?

student toward the discovery of their own individual pathway (Bartlett & Naismith, 2020; Bennett, 2013; Boud et al., 2001; Cremata, 2017, 2019; Hughes, 2010, 2017; Joubert & Schubert, 2016; Powell, 2011, Reinhert, 2018). A facilitator guides musical knowledge and offers a shared learning experience where students assist in the learning process. This kind of student-centered facilitation demands openness and curiosity from both the teacher and the student (Cremata, 2017; Hughes, 2017; Holley, 2019; New & Ghafar, 2012; Williams & Kladder, 2019). The facilitator helps to create a space where student opinions and creativity are valued, trust is established, goals are co-established and match assessments, and feedback is collaborative and celebrated (Boud et al., 2001). A collaborative approach in the PMVS aligns with informal learning and can also engender autonomy in students' learning, which can support continued musical growth beyond their college or university learning experiences.

Considering Culture: Diversity, Equity, and Inclusion

When working with popular music, it is important that students and facilitators acknowledge the history of the music, why it is being sung, and the culture in which it is rooted (Baldwin, 2021). Music within the PMVS must be judged in relationship to its own history, just like "cultures must be judged in relation to their own history, and all individuals and groups in relation to their cultural history, and definitely not by the arbitrary standard of any single culture" (Montagu, 1945). Contemporary (popular) music and the spaces where it is taught, by their very definition, defy canonization, but the teaching must be done by engendering a respect for the rich cultural heritage from where the music came (Smith & Shafighian, 2014). Observing the ongoing importance of avoiding hegemony and decolonizing music education spaces of all kinds, while simultaneously promoting democratic and culturally relevant teaching that ultimately leads to self-expression through original work, needs to be the goal (Allsup, n.d.; Hess, 2019; Woodward, 2017). Therefore, discussing, analyzing, and acknowledging the rich history, culture, and traditions of popular music across the entire curriculum can highlight areas of diversity, equity, and inclusion throughout a PMVS and HPME program.

Repertoire: Sharing Responsibilities and Recognizing Individual Goals

Due to the breadth of cultures, decades, styles, genres, and even new or emerging genres in popular music, there is not a single set of repertoire that will serve all students within a PMVS. Therefore, PMVS facilitators need to be well versed in a wide range of repertoire, vocal techniques, styles, and genres, including how they overlap with one another. This includes the openness required to learn about new techniques and styles and ask for help when needed in order to best serve the needs of all students (Bartlett & Naismith, 2020; Hanlon, 2012; Hoppenjans, 2020; Hughes, 2010, 2014; Leborgne & Rosenberg, 2014; Reinhert, 2019).

Additionally, it is often the students who choose and navigate their repertoire choices. Specifics for why a certain song might help a student's journey need to be clearly stated and understood by both student and teacher for the work to be most effective. Repertoire – or even parts of repertoire – can be used to help students discover new styles, techniques, and sounds, and even help them to discover what kind of artist they want to be.

In the PMVS, repertoire might also include original music written by a student. In some cases, this may be the sole focus of studio instruction (Bartlett & Naismith; 2020; Reinhert, 2019). Engaging with a student's original song(s) aligns with how popular musicians learn and offers authentic practices for individual expression, thus supporting relevant music learning (Hess, 2019; Kladder, 2020). Integrating student-created songs supports constructivist approaches to music learning as well, as students build their own knowledge and understanding in facilitated guidance rather than being told what to learn and perform (Cremata, 2017; Garnett, 2013; Hughes, 2017; Rinaldo et al., 2006; Shivley, 2015; Webster, 2011). At the core of this work are exploration, curiosity, and a desire to investigate authenticity and identity without moving toward a safe-haven of "crystallizing" a student's sound too early in their career (Simos, 2017). Providing spaces where students feel empowered to make choices about the repertoire they sing, as well as celebrating their originally composed works, engages them with authentic practices for learning popular music. This approach encourages a diversity of experiences and avoids "schoolification," a process that is often associated with the addition of new modalities into academic spaces (Cremata, 2019).

Technical Voice Skills

Although facilitators need to be well versed in many styles and techniques, it is often not necessary for all PMV students to have all vocal capabilities connected to all genres and styles. Although some students may desire this kind of flexibility in their instrument and have the determination to make it a reality, it should not be assumed that all students will want to pursue this goal (Bartlett & Naismith, 2020; Benson, 2020; Harrison & O'Bryan, 2014; Hughes, 2010; Reinhert, 2019). Regardless, students who seek to use their voice in professional contexts can benefit from an understanding of the biology, science, and technical skills of the voice. Some of this can be learned and explored within the PMVS. However, more can be discovered in a vocal pedagogy class specifically designed for singers of popular music or by using a textbook that speaks to amplified forms of vocal production (Leborgne & Rosenberg, 2014).

Other Skills: Performing and Recording

Whether performing or recording, it is important to understand that commercial and popular music is amplified music (Edwards, 2014; LeBorgne & Rosenberg, 2014; Hoch, 2018; Reinhert, 2019). Essential components in a PMVS curriculum include: (1) demonstrated proficiency singing with, and an understanding of, microphones, (2) an awareness of the feedback loop and how it changes with amplification, and (3) basic skills working within a digital audio workstation (DAW) environment. All of these will help prepare PMVs for work in the music industry (Bartlett & Naismith, 2020; Benson, 2020; Donohue, 2019; Edwards, 2014; Hughes, 2010; Hughes 2014, 2017; Leborgne & Rosenberg, 2014; Reinhert, 2019). The ability to perform with – and lead – a band is also essential for any PMV. This is an important aspect of the study and one which is almost impossible to achieve within the studio setting alone. However, performative aspects related to leading a band can be addressed in tandem within the broader HPME program.

Holistic Assessment

Holistic assessment is that which includes diagnostic (*what might help most*), formative (*adjustments made along the way*), interim (*program specific*), and summative (*review of end goal*) elements. Holistic assessment responds to the work of the student as a whole (Sadler, 2009). Possible ideas for holistic assessment within the PMVS could include engaging students in constructing their own goals and metrics, requiring reflective journaling, co-creating rubrics, requiring recorded song submissions, or giving a form of technical vocal assessment. Combining these elements would engage students with a more holistic assessment that can help them know where their challenges and strengths lie but also help them to navigate their abilities within the world outside academia and move forward in the world as a confident and knowledgeable vocal professional (Joubert & Schubert, 2016; Wiewiora & Kowalkiewicz 2019).

Conclusion

Considering how popular musicians learn, advocating for student choice and voice, empathizing with students' musical backgrounds, integrating opportunities for collaborative repertoire selection, including students' original music, providing opportunities for learning and performing music outside the studio, considering culture, and creating holistic assessments that cultivate real-world experiences are central aspects of building a successful PMVS curriculum (Bartlett & Naismith, 2020; Donohue, 2019; Hess, 2019; Hughes, 2010, 2014, 2017; Joubert & Schubert, 2016; Reinhert, 2019; Scott & Scott, 2017). These suggestions can lead to a PMVS that serves a diverse population of students and empowers facilitators and students to reach success on their own terms.

In the PMVS, some questions one can ask in relation to developing a curriculum based on the curricular framework from Figure 5.1 include:

- **Motivations**: Who are the students, and why are they attending?
- **Challenges**: Are there traditions (cultural or otherwise) that are being mandated by the school that may or may not align with the goals of the HPME voice studio?
- **Interactions**: Is there any kind of discussion about artistic citizenship and culture?
- **Resources**: Are the ensemble, studio, and classroom spaces equipped with microphones and technology endemic to commercial/popular music singing? Do teachers have the required knowledge to teach PMVs?
- **Pedagogies**: What kinds of pedagogies are employed in the studio – and are they aligned authentically with the music that is being learned?

- **Success**: What are the measures of success, and how are they assessed?
- **Value**: Are holistic growth and life-long learning being taken into consideration?

There is a myriad of possibilities when developing and promoting a PMVS in a larger HPME program. However, each institution will be required to adhere to policies that are mandated by accrediting agencies and individual school requirements. It may take some creative thinking to figure out how best to serve the students and the school, but with some time and careful planning, it is possible to find a pathway that serves all students in a manner that benefits their goals and aspirations. This can all be completed while simultaneously adhering to traditions, culture and authentic practices, and pedagogies within the popular music landscape.

Reflection Questions

1. What are some assumptions you have about the relationship between a teacher and student within the voice studio? How might you challenge those assumptions, lean into being uncomfortable, and see what happens if you explore a more student-centered and informal learning approach?
2. How might you re-assess the traditional jury and develop a more holistic assessment?
3. In relation to this chapter, how would you respond to any or all the questions found within this blog post by Jessica Baldwin (2021) (see https://singinginpopularmusics.com/2021/06/16/before-you-create -that-popular-musics-voice-teacher-position/)?
4. What elements of the curricular framework outlined in this chapter do you think would be the most challenging or successful to implement? Why?
5. What can you do to create a culture of inclusivity, diversity, and cultural awareness around popular music singing and within the HPME program?

References

Allsup, R. E. (2008). Creating an educational framework for popular music in public schools: Anticipating the second-wave. *Visions of Research in Music Education*, *12*(1), 1–12.

American Academy of Teachers of Singing. (2009). *Support of contemporary commercial music (nonclassical) voice pedagogy*. http://www.americanacademy ofteachersofsinging.org/academy-publications.php.

Baldwin, J. (2021). Serving the many? *Journal of Singing, 77*(4), 533–536.

Barnett, R., & Coate, K. (2005). *Engaging the curriculum in higher education.* Berkshire: McGraw Hill.

Bartlett, I., & Naismith, M. L. (2020). An investigation of contemporary commercial music (CCM) voice pedagogy: A class of its own? *Journal of Singing, 76*(3), 273–282.

Bennett, D. (2007). Utopia for music performance graduates. Is it achievable, and how should it be defined? *British Journal of Music Education, 24*(02), 179–189. https://doi.org/10.1017/S0265051707007383.

Bennett, D. (2012). Rethinking success: Music in higher education. *International Journal of the Humanities, 9*(5), 181–187.

Bennett, D. E. (2013). The role of career creatives in developing identity and becoming expert selves. In P. Burnard (Ed.), *Developing creativities in higher music education: International perspectives and practices* (pp. 224–244). London: Routledge.

Benson, E. (2020). *Training contemporary commercial singers.* Oxford: Compton.

Boud, D., Cohen, R., & Sampson, J. (2001). *Peer learning in higher education* (1st ed.). London and Sterling, VA: Routledge.

Cremata, R. (2017). Facilitation in popular music education. *Journal of Popular Music Education, 1*(1), 63–82. https://doi.org/10.1386/jpme.1.1.63_1.

Cremata, R. (2019). Popular music: Benefits and challenges of schoolification. In G. D. Smith, Z. Moir, M. Brennan, S. Rambarran & P. Kirkman (Eds.), *The Routledge research companion to popular music education* (pp. 415–428). Abigdon and New York: Routledge.

Donohue, L. G. (2019). *An Essential Collaboration: Teaching the Commercial Vocalist to Interact Successfully with Audio Technology and the Audio Engineer* (Doctoral dissertation, Belmont University).

Edwards, M. (2014). *So you want to sing rock "N" roll: A guide for professionals.* Lanham, MD; Boulder, CO; New York; and London: Rowman & Littlefield Publishers.

Garnett, J. (2013). Beyond a constructivist curriculum: A critique of competing paradigms in music education. *British Journal of Music Education, 30*(2), 161–175.

Green, L. (2002). *How popular musicians learn: A way ahead for music education.* Aldershot: Ashgate Publishing, Ltd.

Hanlon, S. C. (2012). Reviewing commercial music resources: A guide for aspiring singers and vocal professionals [M.A., University of North Texas]. http://iiiprxy.library.miami.edu:10038/docview/1223512046/abstract/A188156E563A4EC8PQ/30?accountid=14585.

Harrison, S. D., & O'Bryan, J. (Eds.). (2014). *Teaching singing in the 21st century* (2014 ed.). New York: Springer.

Herbert, D., Abramo, J., & Smith, G. D. (2017). Epistemological and sociological issues in popular music education. In G. D. Smith, Z. Moir, M. Brennan, S. Rambarran & P. Kirkman (Eds.), *The Routledge research companion to popular music education* (pp. 451–477). Abigdon and New York: Routledge.

Hess, J. (2019). Popular music education: A way forward or a new hegemony? In Z. Moir, B. Powell & G. D. Smith (Eds.), *The Bloomsbury handbook of popular music education: Perspectives and practices* (pp. 29–43). London: Bloomsbury Academic.

Hoch, M. (2018). *So you want to sing CCM (contemporary commercial music): A guide for performers*. Lanham, MD; Boulder, CO; New York; and London: Rowman & Littlefield.

Holley, S. (2019). Coaching a popular music ensemble. *McLemore Ave. Music.*

Hoppenjans, K. (2020). Cross-voice influence: The relationship between the singing voice and the songwriting Voice. *Journal of Singing, 77*(1), 47–57.

Hughes, D. (2010). Developing vocal artistry in popular culture musics. In S. Harrison (Ed.), *Perspectives on teaching singing* (pp. 244–258). Samford Valley, QLD (Queensland): Australian Academic Press.

Hughes, D. (2014). Contemporary vocal artistry in popular culture musics: Perceptions, observations and lived experiences. In S. Harrison & J. O'Bryan (Eds.), *Teaching singing in the 21st century* (pp. 287–302). Dordrecht; Heidelberg; New York; and London: Springer.

Hughes, D. (2017). Art to artistry: A contemporary approach to vocal pedagogy. In G. D. Smith, Z. Moir, M. Brennan, S. Rambarran & P. Kirkman (Eds.), *The Routledge research companion to popular music education* (pp. 177–189). Abigdon and New York: Routledge.

Hughes, D., Keith, S., Morrow, G., Evans, M., & Crowdy, D. (2013a). What constitutes artist success in the Australian music industries? *International Journal of Music Business Research, 2*(2), 60–80.

Hughes, D., Keith, S., Morrow, G., Evans, M., & Crowdy, D. (2013b). Music education and the contemporary, multi-industry landscape. In *Redefining the musical landscape: Inspired learning and innovation in music education XIX ASME National Conference Proceedings* (pp. 94–100). https://search.informit.com.au/documentSummary;dn=715415487007803;res=IELHSS.

Joubert, L., & Schubert, V. (2016). Activating communal creativities for redesigning higher education curricula: Drawing on intercultural experience. In P. Burnard & E. Haddon (Eds.), *Activating diverse musical creativities* (pp. 159–175). London: Bloomsbury Academic, Bloomsbury.

Kaufman, S. B., & Gregoire, C. (2016). *Wired to create: Unraveling the mysteries of the creative mind* (reprint ed.). New York, NY: TarcherPerigee.

Khan, M. A., & Law, L. S. (2015). An integrative approach to curriculum development in higher education in the USA: A theoretical framework. *International Education Studies, 8*(3), 66–76.

Kladder, J. (2020, October). Songwriting in modern band? *College Music Symposium 60*(2), 1–22. College Music Society.

Lebler, D. (2007). Student-as-master? Reflections on a learning innovation in popular music pedagogy. *International Journal of Music Education, 25*(3), 205–221. https://doi.org/10.1177/0255761407083575.

Lebler, D., & Weston, D. (2015). Staying in sync: Keeping popular music pedagogy relevant to an evolving industry. *Journal of the International Association for the Study of Popular Music, 5*(1), 124–138.

Leborgne, W. D., & Rosenberg, M. (2014). *The vocal athlete* (1st ed.). San Diego, CA: Plural Publishing, Inc.

Moir, Z., Powell, B., & Smith, G. D. (2019). *The Bloomsbury handbook of popular music education: Perspectives and practices.* London: Bloomsbury Academic.

Montagu, A. (1945). *Man's most dangerous myth: The fallacy of race.* New York: Columbia University Press.

New, K. H., & Ghafar, M. N. A. (2012). Self-awareness and social change in higher education. *World Journal of Education, 2*(1), 25–38. https://doi.org/10.5430/wje.v2n1p25.

Powell, B. J. (2011). *Popular music ensembles in post-secondary contexts: A case study of two college music ensembles* (Doctoral Dissertation). http://iiiprxy.library.miami.edu:10038/docview/879778077/abstract/B8745CEC5854470PQ/10?accountid=14585.

Reinhert, K. (2018). Developing popular music programs in higher education: Exploring possibilities (Scholarly Repository). https://scholarlyrepository.miami.edu/oa_dissertations/2057.

Reinhert, K. (2019). Singers in higher education: Teaching popular music vocalists. In Z. Moir, B. Powell & G. D. Smith (Eds.), *The Bloomsbury handbook of popular music education: Perspectives and practices* (pp. 127–140). London: Bloomsbury Academic.

Rinaldo, V., Sheeran, T., Vermette, P., Smith, R. M., & Heaggans, R. (2006). Active learning: A hybrid approach. *Journal for the Practical Application of Constructivist Practice in Education, 1*(2), 1–24.

Sadler, D. R. (2009). Transforming holistic assessment and grading into a vehicle for complex learning. In G. Joughin (Ed.), *Assessment, learning and judgement in higher education* (pp. 1–19). Dordrecht: Springer Netherlands.

Scott, J. C., & Scott, D. (2017). The portfolio career in practice: Key aspects of building and sustaining a songwriting and performance career in the digital era. In J. A. Williams & K. Williams (Eds.), *The singer-songwriter handbook* (pp. 191–206). New York: Bloomsbury.

Shively, J. (2015). Constructivism in music education. *Arts Education Policy Review, 116*(3), 128–136. https://doi.org/10.1080/10632913.2015.1011815.

Simos, M. (2017). The performing songwriter's dilemma: Principles and practices. In J. A. Williams & K. Williams (Eds.), *The singer-songwriter handbook* (pp. 17–34). New York: Bloomsbury.

Smith, G. (2013). Pedagogy for employability in a Foundation Degree (Fd.A.) in creative musicianship: Introducing peer collaboration. In H. Gaunt & H. Westerlund (Eds.), *Collaborative learning in higher music education* (pp. 193–198). Farnham, UK: Ashgate.

Smith, G., & Shafighian, A. (2014). Creative space and the 'silent power of traditions' in popular music performance education. In P. Burnard (Ed.), *Developing creativities in higher music education: International perspectives and practices* (pp. 256–267). London, UK: Routledge.

Smith, G. D., Moir, Z., Brennan, S., Rambarran, S., & Kirkman, P. M. (2017). *The Routledge research companion to popular music education.* Abigdon and New York: Routledge.

Webster, P. (2011). Constructivism and music learning. In R. Colwell & P. Webster (Eds.), *MENC handbook of research on music learning, vol. 1* (pp. 35–83). New York: Oxford University Press.

Wiewiora, A., & Kowalkiewicz, A. (2019). The role of authentic assessment in developing authentic leadership identity and competencies. *Assessment and Evaluation in Higher Education, 44*(3), 415–430. https://doi.org/10.1080/02602938.2018.1516730.

Williams, D. A., & Kladder, J. R. (2019). *The learner-centered music classroom: Models and possibilities*. New York: Routledge.

Williams, J., & Williams, K. (Eds.). (2017). *The singer-songwriter handbook*. New York: Bloomsbury.

Woodward, S. C. (2017). Social justice and popular music education: Building a generation of artist impacting social change. In G. D. Smith, Z. Moir, M. Brennan, S. Rambarran & P. Kirkman (Eds.), *The Routledge research companion to popular music education* (pp. 139–150). Abigdon and New York: Routledge.

6 You Want to Play John Mayer?

Considering Rock Bands as Learner-Centered Music Making in Higher Education

Jonathan R. Kladder

Setting the Stage: Forming an Understanding of Student Interests

A central identifier to teaching popular music in formalized institutions builds upon the notion that musicians already hold a vast understanding of music prior to enrollment in a college or university music program. This directly impacts our role as music educators in the learning experience. Rather than assuming we must impart our musical knowledge to our students, it means that we take on a variety of roles with our students, including songwriting, producing, performing, and learning music as *co-musicians*. Thus, our role is to facilitate a space where students' previous music experiences are validated and included in the studio, classroom, and ensemble experiences at our institutions. As Marcel Proust wrote, "The real voyage of discovery consists not in seeking new landscapes, but in having new eyes" (The Captive, 2019). Proust wrote this broadly, but when offered in the context of this chapter, I believe it holds merit in shifting our role from "teachers" to "coaches" and "facilitators" in the pop/rock performance context.

Co-Creators: Facilitator and Coach

Having new eyes begins by embracing a different role as an educator: one who coaches and facilitates a music learning space (Cremata, 2017). This responsibility recognizes that we are on a musical journey of discovery together with our students. In this modus, instructors are not the "all-knowledgeable" constructors of knowledge but rather co-journeyers and fellow musicians with our students. This holds contrast to much of the music made in higher education, as many musicians on college and university

DOI: 10.4324/9781003216728-7

campuses are either excluded from music making altogether or do not see themselves in the music being performed, as music is often delivered through a teacher-directed and hierarchical power structure (Bradley, 2006; Benedict et al., 2015; Hamilton, 2021). This issue has been at the forefront of many publications and conferences in recent years, with scholars and researchers exposing a hegemony of music making in higher education: a social justice issue that exposes institutional racism in music programs across the US (Palmer, 2011). If we recognize that popular musicians are in fact musical and hold vast musical skillsets, then coaching and facilitating a pop/rock ensemble supports a concerted effort in breaking down barriers related to access in music making across the higher education landscape (Smith, 2016). Furthermore, if we seek to validate all forms of musicianship in higher education, then collectively we can recognize that students bring a wealth of music experiences that would effectively support a relevant and meaningful learner-led and collaborative music making experience (Kladder, 2021). This truth holds significant value in understanding students' contribution to the foundation of music learning in a pop/rock ensemble as well.

As Chapter 1 mentioned, a co-constructed learning environment is built upon evaluating, listening, and creating a learning environment where students' prior knowledge is recognized and incorporated into the learning space. In this modus, all members of the ensemble have equal voice in contributing musical ideas. Often, a band leader will typically emerge. This person is often motivated to assist in organizing rehearsals, both the repertoire and rehearsal process. The first step in creating an environment that is constructed mainly by – and with – the students is to take stock of their musical experiences. Students generally open up about their music making most effectively after they have had an opportunity to meet their partnering musicians, learn about one another, and make new connections. For this reason, we make every effort to instill a culture of openness, vulnerability, and respect from the first rehearsal. The approaches for this may include group discussions at the beginning of each rehearsal, informal jam sessions, online forum discussion spaces, and one-on-one discussions with each musician. Regardless of the approach that is taken, developing relationships – healthy ones – that reflect an openness to musical ideas across a diversity of different musicianship styles is a significant indicator of success.

Setting Course Student Learning Objectives, Assessments, and Repertoire

One of the main goals when designing a learner-led ensemble environment is to connect students' lived experiences to the rehearsal space. This begins by setting relevant student learning outcomes (SLOs) at the beginning of the semester. Sometimes it is feasible for students to co-create student learning objectives in collaborative spaces with facilitated guidance by the instructor. Usually, this can happen on the first or second day of class. Another approach is to offer an online space for collecting ideas using Canvas, Moodle, or Google Forms. It may not be feasible in all contexts for students to write SLOs entirely. However, some students might emerge as leaders or show significant interest in co-writing SLOs. I use the following perspective to guide the process:

> Education either functions as an instrument which is used to facilitate integration and the younger generation into the logic of the present system and bring about conformity or it becomes the practice of freedom, the means by which [humans] deal critically and creatively with reality and discover how to participate in the transformation of their world.
>
> (Freire, 2000, p. 34)

I seek to co-create an ensemble experience that supports the practice of musical freedom, where students apply critical thinking, analysis, creativity, discovery, and the transformation of musical ideas, concepts, skills, and music making in the ensemble space. Therefore, I suggest that the formation of SLOs be critically examined by asking the guiding question: As an instructor, am I am seeking to bring about discovery, transformation, and creativity in the ensemble or uniformity and conformity? These guiding tenets can help write meaningful SLOs that are embedded in constructivist principles and support relevant learning in ways that engage students throughout their music making experience. I want to support opportunities where students bring their individual interests and desires into the music making process, while creating space for them to transform their musicianship into life-long enjoyment and participation in the arts. Students in the rock ensembles I have coached appreciate when we co-write SLOs and evaluate, analyze, and discuss whether they feel the objectives are clear and manageable. A range of student learning objectives are provided below. These SLOs have been used in many pop/rock ensembles and offer a range of different approaches to how they may be structured:

SLO 1: Discover and perform intermediate to advanced techniques in popular music, which includes playing by ear and notational tools such as lead sheets, chord charts, or tablature.

SLO 2: Evaluate, synthesize, and discuss several popular music styles.

SLO 3: Transform musicianship through professional and positive attitudes in fostering a creative and productive learning environment.

SLO 4: Create and perform music in social-collaborative spaces with other musicians in rehearsals.

SLO 5: Discover professional skills in utilizing music technology, including MIDI controllers, sound board management, microphone techniques, tone control, amplified instruments, and live sound reinforcement.

SLO 6: Showcase an ability to manipulate instrument or voice, as appropriate to the repertoire, with respect to accuracy, fluency, articulation, intonation, breath control, fingering, tonal variety and/or consistency, dexterity, tempo, dynamics, etc.

SLO 7: Make sensitive and musical performance decisions, resulting in a transformation of individual interpretative skill, so that the music is performed in a manner reflecting a degree of sensitivity and empathy, musical personality and ensemble awareness; the ability to adapt to a variety of styles may be required by the choice of repertoire.

SLO 8: Discover and create original music within the assigned group.

Typical courses will outline four to five SLOs at the beginning of the semester. Depending on the context and the goals of the pop/rock ensemble, these SLOs can be adapted, modified, or changed as needed.

Assignments and Repertoire Selection

Assessments in a pop/rock ensemble might take a variety of different forms. Importantly, they should always be created using a growth mindset notion of musical learning. Understanding the musical background of each student at the beginning of the semester is essential. I always begin by asking basic questions to gain an understanding of their previous musical knowledge. At the beginning of the semester, I recommend hearing each musician individually. I use a baseline assessment as a means for understanding their musical background and ask students these guiding questions at the beginning of the semester in a brief interview:

1. What instrument(s) do you play?
2. How have you learned how to play them?
3. What experiences do you have playing in a pop/rock band?
4. Do you have any samples of your work, whether multitracked recorded in a DAW or live performance recordings?
5. What chords and scales do you know how to play?

From there, we hold an informal audition, where I hear each student play a musical selection or a portion of music repertoire they have either written or covered. I document their musical ability and knowledge using a qualitative approach. This forms a baseline understanding of each student. In conclusion, I ask students to write four musical goals they would like to achieve over the semester. They then form a plan and a mechanism to meet these goals. The "assessments" I use typically fall "outside the lines" of a traditionally conceived assessments, and we aim to build an understanding of individual musical growth for each musician. I build opportunities for students to showcase their musical growth through something called a *musicianship showcase*. Students arrange a time to play, sing, perform, or share a recording throughout the semester using a new genre, style, or technique they have learned. We embed four to six musicianship showcases throughout the semester so that students have a minimum of four opportunities to demonstrate musical growth.

Repertoire selection is simple, and can take three different approaches: (1) build a repertoire set *with* all musicians as equal members of the ensemble, (2) choose the repertoire for students in the ensemble, or (3) foster an ensemble experience where students choose, discuss, analyze, and synthesize the selections entirely on their own. If we take a constructivist approach to music learning, then using a democratic approach is the most obvious pathway. The methods for selecting repertoire *with* students are relatively straightforward. Collaboratively with the instructor and ensemble members, a collective theme or series of goals are established. Guiding questions in deciding a theme or series of goals might include:

1. What musical goals does the ensemble have, and how might the repertoire selection support efforts to achieve them?
2. Is there a community concert or community project the ensemble might engage with?
3. How might the repertoire provide a meaningful and relevant effort to support this endeavor?
4. How could the repertoire selection bring about awareness of social justice issues in contemporary culture, and how could the song selection bring these issues to the forefront?
5. Will the culminating experience include a live performance, or will it be recorded in fixed media?

In this process, the intentions are to foster critical thinking about *why* the proposed repertoire is being selected. Haphazard selections, ones that are chosen, "just because I like that song," are not the most appropriate choices. Using artists in the commercial music medium as examples is a good approach in supporting students' understanding of how, why, and what songs are selected. In this modus, ensuring student ownership and facilitated guidance are vital for success.

The Integration of Intentional Practices in Institutional Learning

For many instructors in higher education, our musical training and backgrounds are rooted in traditional conceptions of what it means to teach and perform music. Most of us have been modeled, in many ways, a top-down, hierarchical approach to music instruction: the instructor is the "all-knowing" depositor of information, the "master" from whom all knowledge must be gained. This is commonly referred to as the "master-apprentice model," commonplace in music teaching and learning (Heuser, 2014). For most of us, this means that we have been trained to institutionalize music instruction, and often reciprocate a similar approach. The institutions and educational policies that are in play in the US often support, or even honor, this form of instruction. However, recent publications have produced a critical mass of awareness related to issues of "methodized" or "schoolified" instruction (Cremata, 2019a, 2019b), as these approaches may be antithetical to meaningful music learning. Importantly, they may be misaligned with *how* music making has existed around the world and throughout cultures (Green, 2002). As Cremata (2019a) postulated, popular music is becoming more commonplace in formal learning contexts, and in this process, there is a danger that we may strip popular music "from its authentic cultural context and place it in a foreign one" (p. 417). We must continually interrogate our practices, both as instructors and as fellow musicians, to ensure we do not fall into this trap.

First, interrogate your teaching practices regularly. Consider what resources are in place to support the learning process. As mentioned earlier in this book, challenging yourself by continually asking "Why?" and "Is this the most culturally affirming and constructivist approach to music learning?" is an effective method for interrogating your teaching practices. It has become easier, perhaps now more than ever, to find popular music materials "such as method books and curricular guides" (Cremata, 2019b, p. 2). However, "while potentially helpful to teachers and students alike, [they] might be ill-suited to capture the nuances of popular music" (Cremata, 2019b, p. 2).

Second, reflect on the amount of listening we do as instructors. Listening can be difficult for many of us in the profession, with looming deadlines and limited course meetings. We often feel a time crunch while in search of a well-constructed performance. However, listening to our students is vital and supports an effective understanding of their musical needs and interests.

Third, integrate reflection into daily routines. Reflection practices are important for the students in the group, and also for the coaches. Although ensemble experiences are often focused on musical performances and performance preparation, reflection practices have been seen as a significant adjunct to creative disciplines, particularly in music.

As Barton (2015) suggested, reflection is "central to meaningful engagement with a discourse around creative work" (p. 1). In this modus, all participants in the experience are able to deconstruct and reconstruct their musical experiences, make personal, social, and cultural connections between their experiences with the music making process, and engage with musicians in their group. The following four Rs are adapted from Barton's (2015) Model of Reflection. When applied to music, they offer an effective means of developing an environment for reflection that focuses on developing the whole musician (adapted from Barton, 2015):

1. **Reporting and responding** – questions might include:
   a. What experiences were supportive of my musical development?
   b. What experiences provided creative flow-state?
   c. How did I evaluate the group's progress?
   d. What key accomplishments occurred in the rehearsal?
2. **Relating** – questions might include:
   a. How did my progress relate to my peers?
   b. How did my musicianship development support my peers?
   c. How did our group rehearsal develop new skills?
3. **Reasoning** – questions might include:
   a. How can I continue to learn new music terminology to support music making?
   b. How do critical listening and analysis support our group's musical development?
   c. What elements of the rehearsal might I be better prepared for?
4. **Reconstructing** – questions might include:
   a. How can I use these new experiences in future rehearsals?
   b. How can I provide more effective approaches to increase creative flow-state?
   c. What new skills might I use to better evaluate the group's progress?
   d. How do I take key accomplishments and build upon them for future rehearsals?

The following are questions for coaches or facilitators of a pop/rock ensemble:

1. **Reporting and responding** – questions might include:
   a. What experiences were supportive of students' musical development?
   b. What experiences provided creative flow-state?

    c. How was I evaluating the group's progress?
    d. What key accomplishments occurred in the rehearsal?
    e. What was my role in the rehearsal?
2. **Relating** – questions might include:
    a. How well did students' musical progressions relate to each other?
    b. How did students' musicianship support one another?
    c. Did the group develop new skills, and if so, how?
3. **Reasoning** – questions might include:
    a. How can I continue to learn new music terminology with students to support music making?
    b. How was my critical listening and analysis supporting the group's musical development?
    c. What elements of the rehearsal might I support more effectively?
4. **Reconstructing** – questions might include:
    a. How can I support new experiences in future rehearsals?
    b. How can I support more effective approaches to increase students' creative flow-state?
    c. What do I need to do to better evaluate the group's progress?
    d. How do I take students' key accomplishments and build upon them for future rehearsals?

Fourth, associate music learning with intentional practices. What is intentional practice in music ensemble learning? Put simply, intentional teaching practices mean we think before we (re)act. The following attributes might guide our thinking in how we can intentionally guide a pop/rock ensemble experience in higher education. First, ask questions about the rehearsal process to guide thinking in this modus. For example, are we: (1) investigating how things work musically through active exploration of sounds and ideas, (2) establishing healthy relationships and effective communication on our own with minimal assistance, (3) able to discuss and collaborate with one another for assistance when an issue arises in a rehearsal, (4) motivated to solve musical or non-musical problems, (5) able to achieve a creative flow-state so that the instructor's intervention would interrupt them, (6) challenging each other in ways that help achieve and even master new skills, and (7) applying existing knowledge in new ways (adapted from Epstein, 2007)?

Each of these questions supports intentional facilitation in the pop/rock ensemble experience. When interrogating best practices, I suggest considering the following principles:

1. Build trust with musicians in the group, this develops respect between students and coaches, which will also take time to develop.

2. Take time to listen, in the ensemble rehearsals and outside the rehearsal space. Be cognizant and aware of whose voice you listen to more than others. Are you creating a space where all musicians, regardless of ethnicity, musical background, or personality, are able to think and speak safely?
3. Consider responding to student inquiries with higher level thinking questions that help them apply, analyze, and synthesize their experiences in meaningful ways (adapted from Schiller, 2007).

The combination of these three approaches supports a design where constructivist approaches to music learning may succeed in a pop/rock ensemble setting (see Figure 6.1).

Monolinguistic Musical Language Emerges as Multilinguistic in Rehearsal Spaces

Communication between group members is integral not only to their success, but also in building a supportive environment where students are able to effectively learn and perform music cohesively. As popular musicians are often informally trained (Green, 2002), some musicians may not understand formal music terminology or read standard notation. Their approaches to discourse may be different from one another. For example, a popular musician often experiments with a variety of musical ideas without musical terminology that is understandable to some formally trained musicians. It is not uncommon to hear popular musicians "messing around" with guitar riffs, drum fills and beats, or various melodies, trying ideas out, tossing them out, and then recreating or experimenting with another idea. From

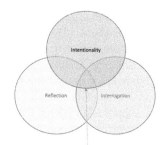

The "intersection" of effective facilitation for best practices in pop/rock ensemble experiences.

Figure 6.1 A visual representation for integrating principles of best practices in pop/rock ensemble coaching in higher education.

an outsider perspective, this "messing around" may be perceived as unorganized, or even haphazard. From an instructor's perspective, it might be observed as accomplishing very little. However, it is important to recognize that this is an approach to music making that is relevant and genuine to creating and performing music in this medium (Green, 2002; Jaffurs, 2004; Kladder, 2021).

Informally trained musicians may not "speak" the language of those who have formal training in music: they are essentially monolinguistic musicians – often well versed in discourse that relies on exploration, listening, and ear-based approaches. Take, for example, an electric guitar player who reads music using tablature, but not traditional staff notation. This musician "thinks" their way of knowing, recognizing tablature as fret numbers, string representation on a guitar fretboard, with no rhythmic representation. In this context, the guitarist will take their time to listen to a recording, or simply play from memory how a particular chord, guitar riff, or melodic figure should be played. This represents a single form of learning and performing music, in a discourse that is often self-taught.

Conversely, a classically trained guitarist may understand how to read staff notation and move fluently around the fretboard. They might sight read material that does not rely on a recorded track or memory of a particular chord, guitar riff, or melodic figure. This musician understands how to communicate with other formally trained musicians, using terminology from the Western European art tradition. They understand accidentals, various rhythmic terminologies, tonal modes, and a variety of meter designations. However, they may not play music by ear, may not explore melodic or chordal structures through "messing around," and may rely on notation for music performing. This form of musicianship is also monolinguistic. Understanding and respecting all forms of music making and learning in a pop/rock setting are integral to supporting students' full musicianship potential and expanding their ability to communicate and perform across a myriad of different contexts and rehearsal spaces. Recognizing this truth can sometimes be a difficult challenge for formally trained musicians, particularly instructors, who see an upcoming performance or looming deadline.

The intersections, or "collisions," between informal and formal musicians pose interesting insights into the pop/rock ensemble space (see Figure 6.2). It offers a space for the emergence of multilinguistic musicianship to coexist, where all approaches to music making are embraced and supported. It relies on a variety of stakeholders who hold similar philosophies related to the importance of both breadth and depth in music making.

It is possible for diverse forms of musicianship to coexist and work cohesively when making music. In this modus, two forms of musicianship would "collide" and collaborate. All members of the group would ideally

Figure 6.2 The collision and intersection of two opposing previous music experiences creates opportunities for collaborative learning.

support and teach one another. This, however, is often a utopian view, and is often not the case. Instead, as two forms of musicianship merge into the same space, increasing the facilitation of the group is often warranted. Coaching, guiding, and supporting the dialect between these musicians is central in determining the group's success. Teaching key terms and musical understandings from both perspectives is vital. Furthermore, as a coach, knowing and understanding both worlds as a musician is equally important. Translating musical language between these two worlds is a significant factor in determining the group's success. From personal experience, there are some approaches that can assist in assuring the coach's or facilitator's role supports these diverse backgrounds in music:

1. Incorporate individual musical goals for all students that embrace a diversity of approaches. For example, formally trained musicians should work to learn music solely by ear; informally trained musicians should begin to learn basic standard notation and key terms associated with Western Classical music.
2. Model basic approaches to music learning from both Classical and popular designations; Use basic rhythmic terminology in ear-based methods, and also Western Classical music notation (write rhythms on a board, for example).
3. Translate often and consistently. Begin by asking the ensemble whether they can explain, define, or translate a musical term or concept.
4. Describe music using a variety of terms from both musical worlds. For example, "loud" and "soft" can also be described in the context of music notation using "piano," "forte," or similar terminology.

Integrating these approaches can assist in a more seamless and smooth collaboration between informal and formal music making dialects. The central goal should remain focused on students' independent musical growth, regardless of their musical background. Although each musician will have a different background, realizing that music can be experienced differently and described through a variety of linguistic approaches is fundamental. More importantly, there should not be a hierarchy in music, but rather a recognition that all musics are valid, and all students should learn a variety of approaches to making music.

In addition to these challenges, creating a space where students can be honest with each other in a manner that is respectful is also important. As commercial and popular musicians enroll in pop/rock experiences in higher education, they sometimes bring opinions about the music they would like to create – and why. At times, these opinions can create conflict with other musicians in the same group who hold different views. To alleviate these tensions, when students create repertoire lists, it is often advisable to create song lists where everyone in the band has an opportunity to learn and perform a song they have chosen. This way, one band member does not feel excluded from the decision-making process and all members of the group feel valued. Sometimes, a coach may need to intercede in ensuring equal representation of all ideas in the rehearsal space. A similar conflict can arise if musicians embrace different sets of values or goals for the music making experience. To remedy this issue, having open conversations with all band members regularly and sharing these goals with one another can assist in creating a space where all members of the group understand the diversity of goals represented in the band. This requires healthy relationships with the coach and each band member. It also requires all members of the group to respect one another, listen, and respond appropriately.

Finally, students with different levels of abilities can sometimes cause conflicts within groups. A more "advanced" player might become frustrated with less "advanced" players. Mistakes are expected, but sometimes too many mistakes create frustration and irritation for those who aim for quick perfection. For this reason, I suggest that each musician has an opportunity to meet one-on-one with the coach prior to the group being formed, as mentioned earlier in this chapter. It is important that the coach understands each musician's previous musical background, abilities, and performance experiences in popular music. Encourage students with the opportunity to submit a short portfolio prior to forming groups. If more than one section can be created (multiple groups within one section is another approach if you have enough musicians), then dividing the groups based on ability could be an option. Sometimes, a one-on-one conversation between a frustrated or irritated student and the coach will be necessary as well. A plan of action to remedy the situation can be made together. Regardless, there are benefits to mixing ability levels, as students can learn from one another, teach one another, and in some cases, students with lower performance abilities or skillsets in popular music can be motivated to practice their instrument more regularly and in turn be pushed to higher levels of musicianship. In these situations, the integration of the coach is central: guiding, listening, and mentoring all musicians throughout the entirety of the process regardless of their musical backgrounds or previous music making experiences. Learning how to work with a variety of musicianship abilities is central to success in the music industry.

Conclusion

It can be a challenge for instructors to embrace a role that is more "guide-on-the side" when coaching a pop/rock ensemble. However, the importance of intentionality, personal reflection, and consistent interrogation of the learner's environment will more effectively support a pop/rock ensemble experience that is relevant to students' interests and built upon prior music experiences. The goal should always remain focused on creating a learner-led environment, including repertoire selection and rehearsal space, where students learn to be multilinguistic musicians, build new musical skills and knowledge across a range of styles and genres, and support individual musical growth. Although challenges can arise, fostering open communication and a relationship of trust between all stakeholders will ensure a successful experience for everyone.

Reflection Questions

1. How might your role as a music educator change in your teaching context? In what ways might you more effectively engage with a "guide-on-the-side", coach, or facilitator role?
2. In what ways might you ensure you are providing a learner-centered music making experience for your students?
3. What challenges do you see in a learner-centered, constructivist approach to pop/rock ensemble leading? How will you overcome these challenges?
4. Outline three strategies that you can take from this chapter that will change or impact your teaching practices.

References

Barton, G. (2015). Reflective practice in music: A collaborative professional approach. In M. Ryan (Ed.), *Teaching reflective learning in higher education.* Cham: Springer. https://doi.org/10.1007/978-3-319-09271-3_5.

Benedict, C., Schmidt, P., Spruce, G., & Woodford, P. (Eds.). (2015). *The Oxford handbook of social justice in music education.* New York: Oxford University Press.

Bradley, D. (2006). Music education, multiculturalism and anti-racism: Can we talk. *Action, Criticism, and Theory for Music Education, 5*(2), 2–30.

Cremata, R. (2017). Facilitation in popular music education. *Journal of Popular Music Education, 1*(1), 63–82.

Cremata, R. (2019a). Popular music: Benefits and challenges of schoolification. In Z. Moir, B. Powell & G. D. Smith (Eds.), *The Bloomsbury handbook of popular music education: Perspectives and practices* (pp. 415–428). London: Routledge.

Cremata, R. (2019b). The schoolification of popular music. *College Music Symposium, 59*(1), 1–3. College Music Society.

Epstein, A. S. (2007). *The intentional teacher* (pp. 734–742). Washington, DC: National Association for the Education of Young Children.

Freire, P. (2000). *Pedagogy of the oppressed.* New York: Continuum.

Green, L. (2002). *How popular musicians learn: A way ahead for music education.* Aldershot: Ashgate Publishing, Ltd.

Hamilton, D. (2021). # BlackMusicMatters: Dismantling anti-black racism in music education. *The Canadian Music Educator, 62*(2), 16–28.

Heuser, F. (2014). Juxtapositional pedagogy as an organizing principle in university music education programs. In Michele Kaschub; Janice Smith (Eds.), *Promising practices in 21st century music teacher education* (pp. 105–124), New York: Oxford University Press.

Jaffurs, S. E. (2004). The impact of informal music learning practices in the classroom, or how I learned how to teach from a garage band. *International Journal of Music Education, 22*(3), 189–200.

Kladder, J. (2021). An autoethnography of a punk rocker turned music teacher. *Research and Issues in Music Education, 16*(1), 4.

Proust, M. (2019). *The prisoner: In search of lost time, Volume 5 (Penguin Classics Deluxe Edition)* (Vol. 5). New York: Penguin.

Schiller, P. (2007). *More Purposeful and Intentional Infant and Toddler Care. Exchange, 178*, 10–13.

Schiller, P. (2009). Program practices that support intentionality in teaching. *Exchange, 185*, 57.

Smith, G. D. (2016). Popular music in higher education. In Ioulia Papageorgi, Graham Welch (Eds.), *Advanced musical performance: Investigations in higher education learning* (pp. 65–80). London and New York: Routledge.

7 Have No Fear, Hip Hop Is Here!

Creating Place and Space for Hip Hop in Higher Education

Thomas E. Taylor, Jr.

Introduction

Providing experiences for students to learn and understand the multifaceted perspectives of hip hop culture in higher education might seem intimidating or overwhelming at first. For some, it reveals challenging questions, such as how do you teach hip hop when you are not a performer, consumer, or producer of hip hop? How might someone learn about hip hop, its history, culture, and influence before teaching it? I would argue that it begins by self-initiated enculturation through active listening and research. Investing oneself in this process develops a respect for, and an understanding of, the value, importance, and influence of hip hop in American culture. I believe we must avoid the fear of not knowing or understanding hip hop enough to develop new college or university courses about it. Finally, I would argue that we can learn along with our students – an attribute embedded into a constructivist approach to learning (Steffe & Gale, 1995).

As hip hop remains the central form of music engagement in popular culture, I believe that music educators should embrace all that embodies hip hop. This is especially true in contemporary culture, where it continues to dominate most of the music produced and consumed today (Kruse, 2016). To advance this notion, I created a course at the University of North Carolina Greensboro (UNCG) and North Carolina Central University (NCCU) called "Topics in Hip Hop." The course was designed so that students' musical interests were central to the curriculum, and since then, the course has created a pathway for sustaining and growing the music program at both institutions. It has also challenged student conceptions related to hip hop in American culture, provided space for students to examine the impacts of racism on Black Americans, and offered a place for deeper reflection about the realities of marginalization for People of Color in the US (Thibeault, 2010; Tobias, 2014). In this chapter, I will showcase how I developed, created, and implemented a hip hop course that explores, investigates, synthesizes,

DOI: 10.4324/9781003216728-8

and analyzes hip hop culture in America. I conclude with implications for the field of music education.

Personal Perspectives and Musical Influences

As a performer, I have existed as a musician in several musical worlds throughout my career, including gospel music, marching bands, classical, jazz, and blues. Each of these have informed my understanding of music making across a variety of contexts. For this reason, I hold multifaceted understandings in music and a deep appreciation for the breadth of music styles and genres in the US. These experiences offered unique perspectives related to music making, which created a personal perspective and realization that popular music, a form of African American and urban music, is a neglected form of music within formal institutionalized learning. Although many schools and universities offer survey courses in jazz or rock, most tend to relegate the originators of that musical genre to a lesser role of importance. From my personal perspective, many jazz or rock courses tend to inflate or add greater attention in the classroom for lesser-known artists. Additionally, some college and university courses avoid controversial topics that create the foundation for truly understanding hip hop – topics that are embedded into hip hop culture and relevant to what students need to understand its influence. This includes issues of social justice like diversity, equity, inclusion, racism, marginalization of particular populations, and crimes against People of Color.

Context and Authenticity: Creating "Topics in Hip Hop"

Authenticity and Relevance

A central tenet in guiding the development of the course was a concerted effort to bridge the musical and cultural chasm that was obvious between students at both UNCG and NCCU and current music course offerings. I also wanted the course to provide opportunities for students to experience the depth and breadth of hip hop: a space and place where they could bring their own musical interests to the classroom and be challenged to critically analyze and synthesize hip hop in social-collaborative settings. These attributes align with a constructivist approach to music learning, as educators who teach using a constructivist design provide students with avenues to connect their lived experiences in the classroom in support of social-collaborative learning and critical thinking processes (Scott, 2011). I wanted students to bring their own music – the music they consumed – to the listening and analysis assignments, so they felt their music was valued and validated (Steffe, 1995).

Classroom Environment

I also wanted the course to show the rawness and beauty of what it takes to create any specific area that I refer to as the four corners of hip hop, which are: (1) DJing, (2) B-Boying, (3) MCing, and (4) Graffiti. Please see Figure 7.1 for an example of Graffiti and the note at the end of this chapter for a definition of each of these.[1] Teaching hip hop culture responsibly requires students to listen and analyze the *original* versions of songs, images, and movies. For this reason, I made a deliberate choice to avoid clean or altered versions of songs that might be available online. I believe that altered versions diminish the overall message, purpose, and intent of the artist. Hearing an unedited version allows listeners to transport themselves to the artist's creative world. Conversely, when the song has been edited and undesired subject matter removed, the message and meaning is often compromised, thus introducing a misinterpretation and misunderstanding of the artist and their message to students. The only way to fully appreciate and understand hip hop begins by experiencing the artists' truth and lived experiences in the manner they present, irrespective of discomfort a listener may feel.

Figure 7.1 The author in front of a Graffiti example used in the Graffiti corner of hip hop. Photo by Thomas Taylor.

It was also important that the classroom was a safe space for collaborative learning and exploration when addressing challenging issues like racism and the marginalization of Black Americans often addressed from within music. Issues like societal oppression and racial inequality are often at the forefront of our discussions. It can be challenging when students know very little about hip hop, racism, and cultural oppression while others may be passionate about it or may have experienced racial oppression firsthand. This dichotomy of varying musical experiences can create uncomfortable spaces, but I often remind students to use polite etiquette and have an open mind. Encouraging open-mindedness significantly assists in creating a safe space for all. For example, the first assignment in the course requires students to watch several hip hop videos on YouTube. Students then discuss how these videos are different from their understanding of hip hop. Nearly all of the YouTube videos in the assignment are of White Women, who are the least likely demographic stereotypically associated with hip hop. I find this encourages students to rethink their preconceived notions of hip hop.

Course Textbook and Assignments

I used a course textbook titled *Yo' Check This: Topics in Hip Hop* (Taylor, 2013) and built class assignments that guided students through a range of hip hop artists and lyric content. The text has proved beneficial for all students, including those who consider themselves hip hop experts, music lovers, or even novice hip hop consumers. This allows students the opportunity to share individualized experiences in relevant ways. In-class conversations and written discussions encourage students to discuss personal perspectives and key takeaways from assignments. In the case of the YouTube assignment, students discuss a variety of observations from the videos, which may highlight other topics that other students did not. For example, some may discuss the fact that mostly women were represented in the videos, while others recognize that they were mostly Caucasian. Some discuss the offensiveness and validity of these videos in general. This encourages students to respond and continue the conversation with one another. I believe this is a crucial point: creating a space where differentiated and authentic learning occurs so that students learn from each other and the instructor.

Institutional Support and Valued Stakeholders

Implementing the course at UNCG and NCCU was relatively simple, as I had supportive administrators at both institutions. From personal experience, the most effective approach to developing a new course in hip hop begins by locating stakeholders who support and advocate for you. In the context of my experiences at UNCG and NCCU, it is probable that without the administrative support I received, the course would have not been as successful. Another reason for my success was that I included a basic outline and timeline in the course proposal, which included a course description, absolutes related to course learning, and student learning outcomes (SLOs). I used the following absolutes in the construction of the course proposal:

> **Absolute 1**: Students are active listeners and will be different listeners than when they arrived.
> **Absolute 2**: Students understand that hip hop is a culture and a way of life, not just a genre of music.
> **Absolute 3**: Students know and understand some of the most influential hip hop artists within the art form, including images, songs of artists, and videos.
> **Absolute 4**: Students must know some of the most influential and important songs, movies, crews, artists, MCs and DJs.
> **Absolute 5**: Students must evaluate and recognize the social justice issues facing our society; this includes students' ability to hear and comprehend the messages in the music, movies, commercials, public speeches, news stories, and conversations included in the course.

As the proposal required constructed student learning outcomes, the following SLOs were used to guide student learning in the course proposal:

SLO 1: Describe how political, social, or cultural systems and structures, in the past or present, have advantaged and oppressed different groups of people.

Description:

1. **Course activities and assignments**: Textbook chapter readings, movie and video assignments that include graded discussions.
2. **Support of SLO 1**: The weekly chapter readings provide initial insight to the oppression and the narrative of revolutionary innovations of people in the cities where hip hop originated. The video and movie assignments provide visual prompts to highlight the cultural, social, and political systems that were established to oppress or impede the people residing in the cities. Reading and viewing assignments with paired quizzes and class discussions teach students to describe their own intuitions regarding personal experiences and hip hop. The assignments and discussions that are submitted in Canvas provide a platform for students to acknowledge the success documented and connect the oppressive systems from the past to current similar scenarios.

SLO 2: Describe how political, social, or cultural systems, in the past or present, have produced and sustained ideas of difference and, in the face of that, how marginalized groups have meaningfully engaged in self-definition.

Description:

1. **Course activities and assignments**: Music listening assignments, listening tests.
2. **Support of SLO 2**: The weekly listening assignments allow students to better understand the lyrical and musical commentary that addressed the political, social, and/or cultural systems of the past, and help them understand their relevance to the present. Guidance is provided on effective listening skills and developing habits that can improve daily life skills unrelated to hip hop. These activities require students to actively listen and understand the great lengths that the musicians who identified as members of marginalized communities took to create the specific assigned listening examples and develop a heightened awareness of the current musical and social climate.

SLO 3: Examine individual and collective responses for addressing practices of disenfranchisement, segregation, or exclusion.

Description:

1. **Course activities and assignments**: Final cultural analysis paper.
2. **Support of SLO 3**: In consultation with the instructor, students create final papers on topics selected from a list presented to the class. Students submit a graded thesis and outline to assist in the development of the paper. The final paper requires students to connect and analyze the impact of hip hop artists who were excluded, disenfranchised, or segregated, but managed to overcome those hindrances. Every paper must provide empirical evidence of in-depth analysis, personal reflections, and connections to the hip hop artists while exploring the societal reactions and responses in the context of history and current times.

Interestingly, there were no barriers associated with approving and implementing the course at either institution. At UNCG, the course was initially set up as an experimental course. Two years later, it passed the university curriculum committee. Although I did have to complete paperwork for creating the course, it passed unanimously, largely because UNCG was supportive in diversifying the music curriculum. NCCU had a hip hop course many years before I began teaching it, which cleared a pathway and allowed the course I currently teach to pass the curriculum committee easily.

The Curriculum: Musical Selections and Textbook

Musical Selections

As much of the course requires students to listen to, analyze, and synthesize hip hop, it was important that each song, artist, and video covered essential topics in the class. For this reason, I carefully listened to and analyzed all material extensively so the subject matter, course themes, and SLOs for each lesson were clear and built sequentially. I used my personal musical library, guidance from a DJer, and the "Billboard Hot 100" 1978–2000 as guides to confirm the songs and artists selected. This was an enlightening process because it challenged me to set aside personal prejudice. I worked diligently to ensure all lessons and subject matter were connected to the course SLOs. Placing all assignments under the four corners of hip hop (DJing, B-Boying, MCing, and Graffiti) facilitated the process. The song selections and listening assignments were the two most important foundations in course development. I also wanted the number of assignments each week to be reasonable and allow students the depth needed to engage with the topic(s) in meaningful ways. Therefore, I included songs from one year and one video per week. It was difficult to limit song selections and videos to one per week as there were many songs, artists, and movies worthy of inclusion, but many were omitted to keep the amount of required listening and watching to a minimum. I did this to increase the depth of critical analysis required of students for each SLO. A sample list of music selections and assignments used in the course is provided in Table 7.1.

Projects and Assignments

The course projects provided opportunities for students' personal interests to thrive. In the past, my courses encouraged students to create original final projects that focused on the four corners of hip hop. Often, students worked in small groups and selected a specific area of hip hop. From there, they created new works. For example, some created a new song with lyrics, others demonstrated B-Boy dance choreography, and a few created original artworks that showcased Graffiti. These projects demonstrated students' knowledge of hip hop and connected key content learned throughout the course. It has been fascinating to see the collaborative effort of some who demonstrate their DJing skills in the creation of original music. Recently, students wrote short papers analyzing the effect of a chosen artist on the culture of hip hop in America. This type of project has allowed other necessary topics in the class to be met for the university general education guidelines. Below is an example of a recent final project.

Table 7.1 Listening excerpts and assignments used in the hip hop class

Song	Artist	Year
"Roxanne, Roxanne"	U.T.F.O.	1984
"Human Beat Box"	Fat Boys	1984
"Jam On It"	Newcleus	1984
"Five Minutes of Funk"	Whodini	1984
"Friends"	Whodini	1984
"La Di Da Di"	Doug E. Fresh & The Get Fresh Crew	1985
"The Show"	Doug E. Fresh & The Get Fresh Crew	1985
"Rock The Bells"	LL Cool J	1985
"King Of Rock"	Run-D.M.C.	1985
"I Can't Live Without My Radio"	LL Cool J	1985
"Girl"	Too Short	1985
"She's On It"	Beastie Boys	1985
"Eric B. Is President"	Eric B. & Rakim	1986
"My Adidas"	Run-D.M.C.	1986
"The Bridge"	MC Shan	1986
"South Bronx"	Boogie Down Productions	1986
"Hold It Now, Hit It"	Beastie Boys	1986
"Make The Music With Your Mouth, Biz"	Biz Markie	1986
2Paul Revere"	Beastie Boys	1986
"6 'N The Mornin'"	Ice-T	1986
"My Mic Sounds Nice"	Salt-N-Pepa	1986
"Girls Aint Nothing But Trouble"	DJ Jazzy Jeff & The Fresh Prince	1986
"Nightmares"	Dana Dane	1986

Project Instructions: For the purposes of this essay, "cultural analysis" means making

connections between artists we have studied and the cultural contexts in which those artists emerged or circulated. Cultural analysis moves beyond the boundaries of the artist themself to establish links among songs, values, institutions, groups, practices, and people.

Excerpt from a Student Project: At a time when the industry was male dominated, Queen Latifah knew early on that she wanted to be her own boss and make decisions for herself because she didn't want a man dictating what she should or shouldn't do (Sykes, 2014, p. 82). Every artist wants the chance of creative control when it comes to their brand, music or anything that their name is associated with. Queen Latifah created her own record company because she had ideas and aspirations of becoming a boss in her own rights. Many artists today have followed in her footsteps and done the same thing. For example, rapper TI has Grand Hustle record label where he manages artists that produce top quality hits. As a rapper he soon realized how lucrative becoming a boss is and has focused more interest in running his record label and completing other ventures outside of music. In a radio interview he stated that music is his first love, but it isn't paying the bills at the moment, so he has ventured into other avenues to stay relevant at a time when album sales are not what they were when he first emerged onto the scene.

Like Queen Latifah, TI has ventured into film, clothing, and management, and television. When you are doing something that you love and enjoy it's easy to give your all. Being able to become a boss is something that takes time, and planning which both have experienced. Entertainers never really know how much time they have in front of the cameras, so embarking on ventures that have the ability to keep you relevant is important. Queen Latifah referenced the individuals around her and stated that, "I think we understood branding a long time ago, and it took a lot of people a long time to catch up to the idea (Norment, 2007)." Thanks to Queen Latifah and her ability to recognize that she can market herself to influence those around her she greatly influenced how hip hop artists view themselves when it comes to branding. For example, Beyoncé has created a brand for herself. She has created business ventures in clothing, shoes, fragrance, and endorsements to name a few that catapults her into the homes of many everyday people. These brands help consumers form an opinion about the artist, as well as the desire to want, use or buy products the artist is promoting. Having the ability to feel as though you can relate to a person is a powerful tool.

This project showcases how one student recognized the impact a hip hop artist had on the culture of being an independent album producer, establishing identity as a musician and producer while impacting the larger hip hop scene broadly. It also showcases the amount of critical thinking and synthesis of facts and listening assignments required across the course. Although this assignment reflects a written assignment, other assignments are based on developing effective critical listening skills as consumers and producers of hip hop. I have found that once students learn how to critically listen and evaluate music in the course, they are able to analyze and synthesize music at a higher level, which supports their understanding of hip hop outside the classroom. This connection to real-world practice is essential in a constructivist classroom, where students engage with critical listening exercises and make connections between classroom learning and real-life experiences (Scott, 2006). In creating projects where students make music, I encouraged them to download a DJ app to experience the challenges and commitment it takes to create original hip hop music. For example, one of the early assignments in the course required students to listen to ten songs by James Brown. I provided the playlist and asked students to pretend that they were the DJ. Their task was to select specific areas from each song and create a new song. In the process, they wrote about the effectiveness of the selected section from each song when they created a new hip hop song. Students used this assignment to support the creation of new music using the DJ app. There are many ways teachers might encourage students to rap or explore the MC element of hip hop in a classroom setting. Although I will make suggestions here, I have learned that most music making processes related to performing or recording hip hop occur outside class. However, in the course, I encourage students to: (1) explore writing lyrics or spoken word, (2) focus on rhythm and pacing when speaking, (3) explore use of voice range so the listener hears the delivered message, (4) focus on rhythm and pacing with a simple beat, and (5) present final performance of the rap/ spoken word.

Course Changes and Developments

After creating the course, I realized the challenge of finding a concise textbook that covered the topics I felt were important and essential in meeting the SLOs. Initially, I used two different books on hip hop. However, these textbooks did not cover the depth or breadth of repertoire needed because they included obscure versions or lesser-known artists performing different songs that replicated the style of the desired song. To remediate this issue, I used my personal music playlist and suggested students use YouTube to find the assigned songs for the class. However, this was fraught with several issues. Students would locate the wrong version by the original artist, find clean versions, select updated versions by different artists, or find remixed versions with different meanings than the original. The importance of students hearing the original message without modification is key to understanding the voice of the artist. The nuance of slang, Urban language, code switching, and metaphors are part of the genius of language in hip hop, and when other versions of a song are used, the meaning of the message tends to change.

In the early years of the course, music streaming services were in their infancy, but growing steadily. File sharing services like Napster captivated America many years earlier, but that approach to releasing music was no longer a viable option. I was seeking a streamlined method of presenting musical examples to the class without breaking copyright laws. To solve this issue, Great River Publishing reached out to me about authoring a hip hop textbook to accompany the class. In 2013, I released a textbook called *Yo' Check This: Topics in Hip Hop* (Taylor, 2013). The text includes a four-month subscription to Napster, and students can listen to any music in the application. This allows students to explore full-length albums in the course and discover new music and artists on their own. The text is offered online, provides a personal understanding of hip hop from the author's perspective, and is a concise reference guide to specific hip hop content, including videos, television documentaries, politics, history, and music. Each chapter has a corresponding quiz, which provides an opportunity to reinforce the subject matter.

Practical Suggestions

Enculturation and Authenticity in Content Delivery

I believe it is fundamental to embrace the culture and music covered in the course. Although it does not mean you must agree with the message in the music, you should develop a greater appreciation of hip hop through a process of enculturation along with students in the course. There are a few steps you can take. First, listen to hip hop as a consumer. Second, research and develop a background of the artists, lyric content, and central messages of the songs. Third, realize that your enthusiasm will be felt and reciprocated in the form of student engagement and participation. I have found that hip hop culture and music emanate a specific energy, and it is important to carry similar energy into your teaching. I have also found that students will embrace excitement about their music, but do not always maintain the same enthusiasm when learning about a new artist or song. Fourth, provide opportunities for students to develop critical thinking skills and social collaboration by facilitating group discussions. Finally, there are often musical, lyrical, or social connections from course content to students' music. Use it to your advantage, because it will help you learn more about their music. Connecting their lived experiences with hip hop is often a viable pathway in creating engaging and meaningful course discussions.

Learning Together: Collaboration

When learning about new artists that students have a passion for, do not hesitate to say you do not know. Sometimes, being transparent is the most effective way to learn together. It is important that you learn together. Sometimes, it is even effective to act as though I do not know a topic, artist, or slang because there is usually another student in the class who also does not know. This situation creates an opportunity for all students to engage and learn from one another. Listen to your students, and when you do, ask them to explain in greater detail. I have found that this energizes students so that they more effectively engage in critical thinking skills and analyze the content on a deeper level. For example, I discuss music using hip hop slang and in course conversations. Slang is used in all hip hop songs, and is a key element in understanding the message within the music. For example, Kurtis Blow has a song called "The Breaks" where he proceeds to introduce the other meanings of the word in "Slang" form (genius.com). In this modus, I ask for the slang word or phrase, the definition, and use it in a sentence so that students understand the word to in a hip hop context. This exercise introduces different ways to analyze and think critically about their familiarity with hip hop language. As the semester progresses, students become more comfortable interacting and assisting each other. Students who work together tend to improve academically. I believe this stems from the continued conversations about the course subject matter outside class, and I have seen the genesis of friendships take place in the classroom from their continued interaction.

Diversity, Inclusion, Equity, and Social Justice: The Hip Hop Connection

The "Topics in Hip Hop" course directly addresses social justice issues and current topics related to diversity, inclusion, and equity. For example, the rawness of unedited songs – ones that include profanity and challenge topics related to racism – is essential to understanding the historical challenges and barriers associated with People of Color in America. At the beginning of the class, I state that explicit content, including the use of profanity and offensive and difficult subject matter, are embedded into the musical examples. I write a disclaimer statement in the syllabus. To reinforce this disclaimer statement, I ask students to read it aloud on the first day of class. The intention to use original and unedited versions of the music exposes the lyrical, musical, visual, and social experiences of the artists so that students are exposed to the challenges and oppression embedded in the music.

The American education system has long avoided topics of racism, oppression, and marginalized populations. However, learning from hip hop offers a mechanism for students to learn about these important lessons and engage with difficult conversations related to racism and oppression in America. Every element of America's success and failures can be seen and heard in hip hop music. There are countless lessons on life, law, finance, civil rights, addiction, and relationships that can be effectively presented using listening exercises, video guides, and class discussions. In each assignment, students are asked to take note of or pay attention to specific portions that speak to oppression, race, and marginalization of particular ethnicities in America. Once they realize the power of the message, they tend to hear or see it throughout the rest of the course. In other words, the ability to truly hear and understand issues of oppression and race creates a permanent awareness.

Conclusion

Starting a hip hop course in higher education can be supportive of efforts to address issues of Diversity, inclusion, equity, and justice (DIEJ) in higher education, can increase access to relevant music experiences from popular culture, and can connect students' lived experiences to formal learning spaces. These types of courses support critical thinking, engagement with the arts, and social-collaborative learning in relevant ways. As the course I developed allows *all* students – regardless of musical backgrounds – the opportunity to learn about hip hop, they are challenged to deepen their appreciation, understanding, and knowledge of hip hop in society and culture.

Hip hop is relevant, meaningful, and imperative for students to learn and respect while creating an awareness about American culture. This holds implications for music teachers, prospective music teachers, and music teacher educators as well. First, it is important that music educators have some awareness of current and emerging music trends. Second, it is imperative that they understand the music that excites their students. For example, creating a hip hop ensemble or including hip hop elements in existing ensembles will bring new and current repertoire that our students will encounter in the music world after school. Third, it is important to develop an awareness and respect for issues of diversity, equity, and inclusion in the music classroom. Learning about hip hop supports this effort, as students engage with difficult discussions related to oppression and race. Fourth, developing the skillset to interpret music in a non-traditional way is essential for a diverse working musician.

Reflection Questions

1. What are two ways you might implement ideas from this chapter into your current teaching situation? How will you accomplish it, and what do you need to do to make it happen?
2. Of the four corners of hip hop, which one(s) did you not know about, and how does this impact your thinking about hip hop?
3. What resources did you find most useful in this chapter, and why?
4. Taylor writes: "As hip hop remains the central form of music engagement in popular culture, I believe that music educators should embrace all that embodies hip hop." Do you agree or disagree with this statement, and why?

Note

1 (1) DJing – the art of creating music in hip hop using multiple record players or turntables with previously recorded music, including sampling and

drum machines, computers, or other electronic instruments. Also often called "Turntablism." (2) MCing – the art of delivering a message in lyrical form in hip hop music by one or more persons. Originally, MC was an acronym of Master of Ceremonies. (3) B-Boying/B-Girling – the art of creating dance in hip hop by one or more persons. The B-Boy style of dancing includes moves from miming, gymnastics, current and popular dance, classical dance (ballet), martial arts, African dance, hambone dance, creative footwork, and improvisation. (4) Graffiti – the art of delivering a visual message in hip hop by one or more persons using spray paint, markers, chalk, found objects, etc. In general, the medium is applied to a space (building, train, sidewalk, etc.) with high visibility so that others may observe and contemplate the message.

References

Kruse, A. J. (2016). Toward hip-hop pedagogies for music education. *International Journal of Music Education, 34*(2), 247–260.

Scott, S. (2006). A constructivist view of music education: Perspectives for deep learning. *General Music Today, 19*(2), 17–21.

Scott, S. (2011). Contemplating a constructivist stance for active learning within music education. *Arts Education Policy Review, 112*(4), 191.

Steffe, L. P., & Gale, J. E. (Eds.). (1995). *Constructivism in education.* Hillsdale, N.J: Lawrence Erlbaum.

Taylor, Jr., T. E. (2013). *Yo' check this: Topics in hip hop.* Dubuque, IA: Great River Learning.

Thibeault, M. D. (2010). Hip-hop, digital media, and the changing face of music education. *General Music Today, 24*(1), 46–49.

Tobias, E. S. (2014). Flipping the misogynist script: Gender, agency, hip hop and music education. *Action, Criticism and Theory for Music Education, 13*(2), 48–83.

8 A Way Forward

Implications and Suggestions for Emerging Music Teacher Educators

Radio Cremata

Introduction

We have a problem in music teacher education. While we do currently have a seemingly functional model that allows for access to and promotion from within its highly guarded borders, it does not allow for diverse musicians or varied perspectives to co-mingle within it (Campbell et al., 2014). Essentially, it functions to self-perpetuate, at the cost of exclusion, many musics and individuals not in the band, choir, and orchestra (BCO) culture. It sequentially promotes membership from within, and is exclusive. For example, children who excel in the study of music from secondary BCO programs are often the limited few who are granted access to a college-level music education where such study is advanced. Those same students graduate and seek employment teaching music to children, which perpetuates a cultural divide between future music educators and future music learners. Consequently, music education, as a profession, is constricted and cannot naturally evolve without deviance or deviators operating with it (Kalio, 2017; Kratus, 2015).

The conservatory model, which privileges particular musicianships, instrumentations, musical styles, and learning approaches, is often the container for music teacher education programs (Williams, 2015). This model is built around exclusive traditions centering on BCO with a smattering of inclusive musics relegated to the periphery such as general music and multicultural music (Allsup, 2003). Contemporary music styles are not well reflected in the conservatory model. As this book advocates, music educators and music teacher educators must be well prepared to teach more diverse cultures with ever-evolving musics, musicianships, and learning styles. This will assist in sustaining and maintaining a strong future for the music education profession. Although there are certainly undeniable benefits to preserving practices, honoring traditions, and curating habits, as a profession, in the US we have been charged by the National Association

DOI: 10.4324/9781003216728-9

for Music Education (NAfME) to be *more* inclusive and serve *all* student cultures more effectively (NAfME, 2021). We must emerge from the past and embrace new horizons.

To do so, we begin by confronting the reality that currently enrolled music education students in undergraduate music education programs will begin employment in no greater than five years. They will have a projected retirement date of 35 years. Therefore, music teachers will need skills associated with those times, which will likely include new musics that are situated and entwined with and around electronics, computers, artificial intelligence, and other machines (O'Leary & Tobias, 2016). Whether we want to admit it or not, our traditions in BCO are outdated, outmoded, irrelevant, and not resonant with contemporary youth culture.

Challenges to the Profession

Currently, music teaching and learning in higher education is well suited to teach musics and musicianships of the past (Kratus, 2007). Mostly, it favors teacher-centered pedagogies with limited emphasis on constructivist approaches. It commonly promotes the teaching of vocal styles associated with Classical music. Only in rare exceptions does it consider the contemporary voice or rapper as a bona fide vocalist. Choral singing emphasizes blending and balancing of voices in favor of a unified group sound that is often not mixed, microphoned, or amplified using live sound technology. In instrumental contexts, string, wind, and percussion players are taught apart from vocalists and have their own instrumental ensembles (big and small). In unique circumstances, they are combined with vocalists for special performances. This musical isolation and separation, while common in Classical music, is not reflective of contemporary music making contexts. Moreover, it does not focus on process-over-product music learning, facilitated instruction, or individual creativity (Cremata, 2017; Kanellopoulos, 2021).

In most classrooms, music is learned using standard notation. This grants access to a specific type of music learner who has likely been promoted through an environment that favors drilled repertoire, methodical learning, and sequential skill building. Such paper-based musics perpetuate "schoolified" music learning that is designed around commercialized distillations for the primary purposes of easing teacher-centered instruction and commoditizing the economy of large-ensemble-oriented profit-bearing music merchants (Cremata, 2019). The musical skills students engage in in BCO rarely diverge from the tradition it seeks to promote. Thus, it continues to be situated within a particular musical heritage that celebrates a narrow and often culturally elitist dimension of music. Instrumentalists and singers in these classrooms are trained in musical fundamentals often solely associated with the Western European art tradition. They are outgrowths of musics from those same cultural lineages. The teaching of that music, whether in a teacher/apprentice, one-on-one, small group, or conductor/ensemble setting, is all a part of the larger musical tradition that celebrates BCO. While BCO is an efficient and economical model for school music in which one teacher can lead a large group of students on musical activities that celebrate uniformity, discipline, and order (all hallmarks of classroom management), the musics themselves represent a small slice of the musical diaspora that precedes us and is operating around us currently (Cremata, 2017). The profession celebrates this with gold medals and rankings, which further deepens the BCO model, as packed classrooms with large numbers of students normalize uniformity and conformity. In fact, larger ensembles are celebrated, encouraged, and desirable. In some cases, they are expected.

However, this approach is counterintuitive to a widely accepted notion that smaller student–teacher ratios in education are more effective in enhancing student learning, supporting creativity, and promoting critical thinking (Klonsky, 2002). It also dishonors individuality and marginalizes students in the process. Particularly, it marginalizes students who do not originate from cultures often associated with large ensembles. The challenge is to find ways for *all* students to engage in new musical styles that not only recognize and honor the various cultural heritages and historical pasts, but also acknowledge and celebrate more recent, contemporary, and emerging musical practices.

I argue that the process of change requires a new kind of music teacher: a teacher who can bridge divides, operate competently within and in between musics of multiple styles, cultures and times, and balance pedagogical approaches that are most appropriately situated within those music experiences. This notion supports the primary goal of this book, which is to provide contexts of innovative and emerging pedagogy and curricula for teaching commercial and popular music in higher education. Change will require an emergent music educator: one who is challenged to be a master of many musics and pedagogical approaches; one who is a thoughtful guide and can support a student's construction of new knowledge in music. An emerging music educator can match students together in ways that create healthy social learning communities that are conducive to musical collaboration.

Opportunities for the Profession

Practitioners can benefit from adapting to change by learning a variety of skills. These may include gaining certifications in computer or music technology-based contexts. TI:ME is one such organization that might be able to help provide additional certifications in established music technology-centered teaching practices. This could happen in the undergraduate or graduate music teacher education curriculum or as part of workshops for in-service teachers. At the same time, those new practitioners might explore new forms of technology learning such as programming, coding, or engineering, which would intersect well with classroom learners (O'leary, 2020). Here, practitioners can expand their palettes of music instruction to include sound engineering and programming. This would likely lead to more project-based learning contexts and student-centered classrooms. While practitioners expand in their technical skillsets, they might also explore deeper understandings in the potential for learner-led pedagogical expressions. This may run counter to conducted classes, but can serve practitioners well as they learn to decentralize themselves from the learning process. The potential to learn those skills exists within music pedagogy classes and beyond, such as in leadership seminars, group dynamics workshops, and chamber music contexts. The more practitioners explore those possibilities, the more likely they may be to employ those teaching practices. They might do well to network on music teacher social media platforms to seek out opportunities to collaborate with peers or learn about ways others lead their classes. This will thus lead practitioners away from ingrained practices and repeated activities in classrooms perpetuated year-to-year, and into seeking new materials/resources to unleash technology-based or learner-led music learning. This will necessitate some political and grant-writing skills needed to make some of these changes possible. Music teachers will do well to explore grant-writing and fundraising as early as in their undergraduate work. For in-service teachers, they could join grant-writing workshops either in their school districts or through resources such as the organization LEARNGRANTWRITING.ORG. In many ways, emergent music educators are entrepreneurs. They will benefit from some business or self-promotion training which could help them better navigate the future of applying for and managing funding and new ventures.

The previous chapters in this book celebrate various innovative and emergent approaches, ones that applaud new possibilities and reconsider pedagogical approaches that decenter teachers, build instruction on students' prior knowledge, and promote musical diversities of various geographical and time-bound cultures. This book has shed light on how emerging music educators and music teacher educators might expand musicianship in higher education, build new understandings of music making across a variety of contexts, and integrate pedagogical approaches that remain outliers in the field of music education.

We learned about the important connection between constructivist learning and commercial and popular music. The benefits of learner-led musical experiences are notable, and may nudge our profession to reconsider the dominant teacher-centered approaches we have historically favored. As such, music learners who are given increased autonomy may bring more diverse musics into their learning contexts – musics that are a better reflection of student interests than the teacher-centered models commonplace in the profession. This might also help bridge school-to-home and home-to-school music learning, thus connecting music to life and the real world.

Musical technologies such as MIDI, digital audio workstations (DAWs), and electronic digital instruments (EDIs) help to promote new forms of musicianship and musical literacy that take us into the future, surpassing traditions which were limited to acoustic music, oral traditions, or notation-based musics. Technology can also give birth to new architectures of musical collaboration between and among musicians in various temporal dimensions, twisting the tapestry of the musical and social fabric that glues together organized sounds (Cremata & Powell, 2017). Humanity has a role in making music with and alongside machines. Music teachers and learners need to be able to explore these opportunities and leverage them as a part of who we are and what we will become.

The musics we teach are reflective of the culture and heritage we celebrate and honor. By intentionally teaching musics such as hip hop, digital, popular, or rock, historically underrepresented musics may find themselves engaged in the music profession in ways otherwise not possible. These types of music are far more representative of contemporary culture and far more accessible, if emergent music educators can find pathways to promote the, at their institutions. The inclusion of often marginalized musics can also further equitize the music learning culture. As an outcome, school music will likely gain greater popularity, students may find deeper interest, and more students may see themselves reflected in the music of those settings (Kruse, 2016). Emerging music educators will need to carefully balance cultural considerations and introduce new musical cultures to their students while building on the heritage they are from. An emergent music educator, one who is willing to bridge these gaps, will naturally run into challenges when making connections. However, these challenges should not discourage us from trying. The potential gains of such an endeavor are ripe with opportunity. Emergent music educators have much to look forward to when embarking on these new opportunities, all the while maintaining a posture that is responsive to their students.

Practical Suggestions

An emergent music educator, by definition, will deviate from current ingrained practices in the profession. In this way, future music teachers will experience music education in new ways. During their developmental years and leading up to their preparation for college, future music teachers cultivate habits, values, and skills espoused by those already in the profession. Music educators can be influential by recognizing their students' personal preferences and habits that define not only who they are, but also what they do and what they wish to preserve (Conway, 2002). These habits are promulgated to their pupils, and serve to define their assimilation and enculturation in music education. In fact, those habits can influence who they determine qualifies as a student at admission to and promotion through their music teacher education programs.

Change begins by taking action (Kratus, 2015). Therefore, I propose a variety of suggestions as a beginning. Although these are just a few of the many possibilities that extend out from a commitment to be an emergent music educator and build upon those suggested in earlier chapters of this book, there are always more. These suggestions for elementary and secondary contexts enable new opportunities for children with technology, and could be used in a variety of elementary or secondary music education method courses as well. At the same time, these technologies might benefit the profession more broadly, because students who are exposed to them could lead the future of music education as well.

To begin, I propose that elementary general music (EGM) introduce various technologies by third grade, because they can provide new pathways to MIDI, DAWs, and EDIs. If early EGM provides sufficient foundational knowledge with creativity and technology, students can explore Modern Band, beat-making opportunities, project-based learning, and learner-led collaborations in upper elementary. To make technology more infused and integrated into EGM, tablets, software, and gestural interface instruments can be used, starting in early stages such as K-2. Teachers can also introduce small problem-based projects that initiate constructivist learning contexts for young students. This can be as simple as small puzzle-like assignments where students reassemble the musical notes to familiar songs using tools like Chrome Experiments' Song Maker used in tandem with Hooktheory's Hookpad. Ideally, similar technologies would be integrated into EGM methods courses for undergraduate students to teach with and experience. While assignments and homework might not be customary at such a young age for students in early elementary music classes, the realistic potential to interact with these free resources at home exists. I recommend that classroom instructors assign homework for this age group with simple assignments such as unscrambling songs in visual puzzle form. Having students do this in class and at home would allow for additional practice and greater facility with the technologies and their aural skills.

At the same time, EGM can develop cultural knowledge that promotes world musics and diversities beyond segregated or homogenous music learning settings. They need not function exclusively as feeder programs for BCO. EGM possesses great potential at various stages of development to engage young music learners with a focus on developing not only better musicians, but also better citizens in a pluralistic society. While exploring various multicultural lesson plan ideas, including those published by Smithsonian Folkways and the Association for Cultural Equity, the same songs can be learned, performed, and celebrated in the music classroom. Assignments at home for this are very feasible. Students might explore a selected or assigned list of musics from those resources. Then they could unpack some correlated historical facts and find related music from that time period. In turn, they could share facts about these musics in class with peers or teach their peers to sing or play those songs in large or small group activities. As diversity is centered on elementary contexts, it may be easier for lessons to deviate away from exclusive BCO paths. Upper elementary provides wonderful opportunities to introduce more than traditional band or orchestra instruments to students. For example, Little Kids Rock offers Modern Band curricula for teaching electric guitar, keyboard, electric bass, drums, pop vocals, and technology as alternative forms of ensembles and music making. Many upper elementary students might enjoy beat-making and hip hop-oriented music experiences, including songwriting and collaborative digital music production opportunities. Assignments for this are within reach. Students could explore Little Kids Rock's Jam Zone (https://jamzone.littlekidsrock.org) at home and learn a song, take a lesson, or practice. The flexibility here to allow students to work at home and connect with familiar popular music which they may be able to stream on services such as Apple Music, YouTube, or Spotify abounds. Students might return to class and share what they have learned, or possibly teach their peers in small or large group contexts.

Secondary music programs in 6th–12th grades offer a broad spectrum of musical opportunities that could be much more than BCO. Since students tend to join new schools at this stage, I suggest that 6th–8th grade students be offered fundamental musical skill experiences that are age-appropriate. This could creatively manifest itself alongside music technology and popular musics. It could also include electronic music making in project-based settings using tools like Ableton, Soundtrap, or Soundation with a focus on creativity. Traditional software tools like Sibelius and Finale could be introduced alongside Noteflight or other web-based tools. This might lead to experiences in songwriting, networked ensembles, machine-music making, audio/video programming, and deterritorialized collaborative musicianship across borders and cultures through and with technologies (Bell, 2016;

Cremata & Powell, 2017). Homework assignments might center on collaboration with peers in other cultures or time zones to encourage a diversity of experiences and challenge learners to make music asynchronously with others. At the same time, students might enjoy virtual music making, such as online jamming, multi-track audio/video recording, or music making with famous artists using pre-recorded videos.

The possibilities for virtual music making are immense (Whiteley & Rambarran, 2016). An assignment in which students collaborate with one or two classmates in self-selected friendship groups might work well for this context. To challenge students on another level, they might multi-track themselves in a 4-square or larger video in which they play or sing various parts of the music alongside a famous artist. Some other ideas might include asynchronous and synchronous online collaboration, virtual ensembles, live looping, Vocaloid, autotuning speech, found sounds, coding, and text-to-speech rap. Each of these can be fleshed out by the classroom teacher, but the potential is very high to showcase the technologies and leverage their attraction to engage learners. I suggest starting simple, with either coding simple mi-re-do melodies, doing text-to-speech rap projects on simple 16-beat grids (finger drumming), or autotuning a short clip of spoken word from the news or television. Secondary music is precisely the time in which most students lose interest in school music, so it would benefit the profession to aggressively pursue and promote innovative, attractive, and learner-centered music learning opportunities that leverage the cultural capital of adolescent life, including the games and musics that inspire them. All of these ideas could be integrated and promoted within a band, string, or choral pedagogy course in music teacher education coursework requirements as well.

Regardless, we must, as a profession, find opportunities for more innovative and relevant music making. If it does happen that BCO becomes less popular and phases out of existence due to increased interest in more learner-led, culturally relevant music education, then music teachers and music teacher education programs will need to adjust to the trends. There is no perfect future, but we must consider new possibilities and think about ways we can challenge our profession to move into the future.

Although each of the aforementioned suggestions could be applied to a host of method courses in the music teacher education curriculum, Table 8.1 offers suggestions for higher education. These suggestions for undergraduate and graduate contexts enable new opportunities for future educators to expand notions of musicianship in contemporary society. Music teacher education programs that promote BCO students will need to deviate and build new experiences in this modus as well. Although there is no single specific roadmap for this, it will necessitate recruiting new kinds of applicants who are not part of the BCO culture.

Table 8.1 Suggestions for emerging changes to music teacher education (MTE)

	Idea 1	Idea 2	Idea 3	Idea 4
Undergraduate MTE	Expand and advance new admissions criteria to include digital musicianship and a diversity of instrumental, and musical styles	Focus on experiential learning with some online learning content	Provide modeling for teacher-led, conducted, facilitated, and informal learning approaches	Update curricula in support of both traditional and contemporary music
Graduate MTE	Expand admissions criteria to allow for new student populations and different routes to certification	Explore more distance learning wedded to field experiences and career learning	Provide dual paths for practitioners and researchers	Consider partnering with other certification programs, such as technology, theatre, and other combinations that might lead to an enriched profession

Additionally, music teacher education programs might require new degree experiences, including facilitated instruction, popular music styles, culturally responsive pedagogy, technology-associated music making, and student teaching in aligned contexts. I recommend an emphasis on closely mentored experiential learning at the undergraduate stage, with an emphasis on breadth over depth in areas that can help promote diverse musicianships and pedagogies. At the graduate level, greater emphasis on field experiences and dual certifications would allow for more nimble professional opportunities. This change will require a commitment on the part of music teacher educators and additional music faculty engaged in those collegiate music education settings. However, once a change is initiated in music teacher education on a large scale that impacts the profession, the three-part PK 12–Preservice–Inservice cycle will showcase new opportunities as well.

Implications and Conclusions

Data suggest decreases in music teaching jobs and BCO student enrollment in the US (Elpus & Abril, 2019). We are left with a choice to make. Are we willing, as a profession, to consider emergent avenues to develop future musicians and music teachers? If the answer is yes, then there is a potential to promote progress and evolve alongside popular culture and innovation. If the answer is no, then the music education profession will not be sustainable as it functions currently. Band cultures derived from antiquated military traditions, choirs from pre-technological settings, and orchestras originating in and dominated by culturally elite aristocratic societies of privilege represent a very small portion of the world's musics and peoples. We need to help right the ship in ways that promote an adaptive music education community in ways that respond thoughtfully and responsibly to a diverse social demand.

Music teacher educators and music instructors in all areas of higher education are part of this equation. Collectively, we need to make more pointed efforts to admit new kinds of music learners to our music programs and provide meaningful college music experiences that further develop and prepare them to teach in diverse musical contexts (Kladder, 2021). To be sustainable and responsive to students and society, the music profession will require future educators who are adaptive, flexible, motivated, self-directed, and capable of change. They will need to be nimble enough to teach diverse musics. They will need to be able to select music and direct their ensembles while standing on podiums, yet at the same time, they will also need to be willing to sit alongside their students and be responsive to them. They will need to be much more than conductors and traditional directors. This may entail a broad level of music instruction stratifying early childhood to 12th grade.

Our profession has a rich history, but it also has a bright future. We are called now to move beyond curatorial habits of antiquated musicianships and turn toward progress, innovation, and emergent musicianships. We would be negligent if we did not rethink our practices and look toward engaging broader groups of learners. By facing forward and addressing the possibilities and potential for new pedagogies and musics to be part of the music education landscape, we can enable a more sustainable and successful music education for the future. I hope that this book serves as a catalyst for the profession to take one step forward in that direction as we seek to expand music education into new possibilities and new musics that better represent the future.

Reflection Questions

1. How can we define emerging music education?
2. Who will be served by emerging music education?
3. What will be some potential challenges to our profession if we move toward emerging music education practices?
4. How can we disrupt the tightly knit cycle of school music in some or all these stages: K12 settings, preservice music education, and in-service music education?
5. What are some examples of emergent music education beyond those suggested in this chapter?

References

Allsup, R. E. (2003). Mutual learning and democratic action in instrumental music education. *Journal of Research in Music Education, 51*(1), 24–37.

Bell, A. (2016). The process of production | The production of process: The studio as instrument and popular music pedagogy. In R. Wright, B. Younker & C. Beynon (Eds.), *21st century music education: Informal learning and non-formal teaching approaches in school and community contexts* (pp. 379–392). Montreal, QC: CMEA.

Campbell, P. S., Myers, D., Sarath, E., Chattah, J., Higgins, L., Levine, V. L., ... & Rice, T. (2014, November). *Transforming music study from its foundations: A manifesto for progressive change in the undergraduate preparation of music majors.* Missoula, MT: College Music Society. http://symposium.music.org/index.php.

Conway, C. (2002). Perceptions of beginning teachers, their mentors, and administrators regarding preservice music teacher preparation. *Journal of Research in Music Education, 50*(1), 20–36.

Cremata, R. (2017). Facilitation in popular music education. *Journal of Popular Music Education, 1*(1), 63–82.

Cremata, R. (2019). The schoolification of popular music. *College Music Symposium, 59*(1), 1–3. https://doi.org/10.18177/sym.2019.59.sr.11433

Cremata, R., & Powell, B. (2017). Online music collaboration project: Digitally mediated, deterritorialized music education. *International Journal of Music Education*, *35*(2), 302–315.

Elpus, K., & Abril, C. R. (2019). Who enrolls in high school music? A national profile of US students, 2009–2013. *Journal of Research in Music Education*, *67*(3), 323–338.

Kallio, A. A. (2017). Popular "problems": Deviantization and teachers' curation of popular music. *International Journal of Music Education*, *35*(3), 319–332.

Kanellopoulos, P. A. (2021). Creativity and 'the contemporary' in music education–A sociological view. In Ruth Wright; Geir Johansen; Panagiotis A Kanellopoulos; Patrick Schmidt (Eds.), *The Routledge handbook to sociology of music education* (p. 377). Abingdon, Oxon; New York, NY: Routledge, Taylor & Francis Group.

Kladder, J. (2021). An autoethnography of a punk rocker turned music teacher. *Research and Issues in Music Education*, *16*(1), 1–38.

Klonsky, M. (2002). How smaller schools prevent school violence. *Educational Leadership*, *59*(5), 65–69.

Kratus, J. (2007). Music education at the tipping point. *Music Educators Journal*, *94*(2), 42–48.

Kratus, J. (2015). The role of subversion in changing music education. In C. Randles (Ed.), *Music education: Navigating the future* (pp. 340–346). New York: Routledge.

Kruse, A. J. (2016). 'They wasn't makin'my kinda music': A hip-hop musician's perspective on school, schooling, and school music. *Music Education Research*, *18*(3), 240–253.

NafME. (2021, June). *Inclusivity and diversity in music education*. https://nafme.org /about/position-statements/inclusivity-diversity/

O'Leary, J. (2020). Music, technology, and education: Critical perspectives, A. King and E. Himonides (eds)(2016). *Journal of Popular Music Education*, *4*(3), 393–395.

O'Leary, J., & Tobias, E. (2016). Sonic participatory cultures within, through, and around video games. In R. Mantie & G. D. Smith (Eds.), *The Oxford handbook of music making and leisure* (pp. 543–566). Oxford: Oxford University Press.

Whiteley, S., & Rambarran, S. (2016). *The Oxford handbook of music and virtuality*. London: Oxford University Press.

Williams, D. A. (2015). *The baby and the bathwater*. College Music Society. Accessed on June 1, 2021 from http://doi.org/10.18177/sym.2015.55.fr.10883.

Index

formal music education 12, 38, 53, 54,
64, 85, 86
four Rs, Barton's Model of Reflection
82–83
freemidi.org 29

Gale, J. E. 12, 13
Gershwin, G. 25
"gigs" 15
Graffiti corner of hip hop 92, *92*, 103n1
Great River Publishing 99
Green, L. 4, 5, 14, 64
"guide-on-the-side" approach 14
guitar, in Apple's GarageBand
application 51, *52*

higher education: change in 19–20;
commercial and popular music in 1–
2, 6–7; constructivist approaches in
16–19; contemporary practice in 36;
exclusive audition requirements in 4;
hip hop culture in *see* hip hop culture
in higher education; learner-centered
music making in *see* learner-centered
music making in higher education;
music teaching and learning in 105
higher popular music education
(HPME) programs 62–64, *63*, 65, 71
hip hop culture in higher education 90–
91, 102; collaboration of 100–101;
context and authenticity of 91–95;
curriculum of 96–100; enculturation
and authenticity in content delivery
100; personal perspectives and
musical influences 91; "Topics in
Hip Hop" course 101–102
holistic assessment 69–70
Hope For Justice, organization 58–59
HPME programs *see* higher popular
music education (HPME) programs
Hyman, D. 25

informally trained musicians 85, 86
"Innovative Teaching Opportunities
with iPads Grant" 51
institution: community 11; learning,
intentional practices in 81–84;
racism in music programs 77;
requirements of 4

integration: of commercial and popular
music in higher education 6, 10; of
intentional practices in institutional
learning 81–84; principles, visual
representation for *84*
intentional facilitation in pop/rock 83
International Justice Mission,
organization 58–59
iPadist 58

Jaffurs, S. E. 5
Jobs, S. 51
Joplin, S. 28, 29

K–12 contexts, commercial and popular
music in 4
Keyboard for the Electronic Musician,
Berklee Online course 44
Kladder, J. 2, 5, 14, 18
Kratus, J. 3

learner-centered approach 33, 56,
57, 59
learner-centered music making in
higher education: assignments
and repertoire selection in pop/
rock ensemble 79–80; co-creators
in pop/rock ensemble 76–77;
integration of intentional practices
in institutional learning 81–84;
monolinguistic musical language
84–88; student interests 76; student
learning 77–79
learner-centered pedagogical
approaches 56–57
learner-led musical experiences
107–108
LEARNGRANTWRITING.ORG
organization 107
Lebler, D. 14
levels of proficiency, EDI program
45–46
limited music teacher education
programs 4
listening approach 18, 32, 77, 81, 88,
90, 91, 95, 96, 98, 101
Little Kids Rock (LKR) 4–5, 110
LKR *see Little Kids Rock* (LKR)
The Love Concert 59